Walking Trails of Southern Wisconsin

CX

W9-AAU-063

Walking Trails
of Southern Wisconsin

Bob Crawford

The University of Wisconsin Press
A North Coast Book

The University of Wisconsin Press
114 North Murray Street
Madison, Wisconsin 53715

3 Henrietta Street
London WC2E 8LU, England

1   2   3   4   5   6   7   8   9   10

Printed in the United States of America

Text and cover: *grw*

Library of Congress Cataloging-in-Publication Data
Crawford, Robert F., 1935–
Walking trails of southern Wisconsin / Robert F. Crawford.
260 p.   cm.
Includes bibliographical references and index.
ISBN 0-299-13840-2   ISBN 0-299-13844-5 (pbk.)
1. Walking—Wisconsin—Guidebooks.   2. Wisconsin—
Guidebooks.   I. Title
GV199.42.W6C73   1994
796.5'1'09775—dc20   93-39165

For Muggsy, Mark, Tracy,
Mary, Tom, and Jenny

Contents

Acknowledgments

I eagerly acknowledge the many people who have helped me assemble information for this book and ensure its accuracy. Special thanks go to Gary Werner, state director of trail planning and protection, Ice Age Park & Trail Foundation, who reviewed the entire manuscript and provided many useful suggestions; and Dr. John W. Attig, associate professor, Geological and Natural History Survey, University of Wisconsin–Extension, who helped with portions about glaciation. Professor John E. Ross, Department of Agricultural Journalism, University of Wisconsin–Madison, also critiqued the manuscript and provided helpful comments.

My thanks also to the many people who work to build and maintain the trails I describe in parks and preserves throughout southern Wisconsin. Department of Natural Resources people who were specifically helpful to me were Dave Hammer, chief of trails, planning, and cooperative programs; state park superintendents Tim Miller, Devil's Lake, Deb Weidert, Lake Kegonsa, and John Wald, Pike Lake; Derek Duane, director, MacKenzie Environmental Education Center; Dave Gjestson, coordinator, Lower Wisconsin State Riverway; Tim Larson, a fisheries manager who supervises the Rowan Creek Trail; and Pat Kaiser, a wildlife manager who talked with me about Mud Lake Wildlife Area.

County and city park directors and others who provided help were Ken LePine, Dane County; Rick Ladine, Kenosha County; Tom Presny, Janesville; Russ Hefty, Madison conservation resource manager; and Cy Wynstrand, Madison parks department. And special thanks to Katherine Rankin, editor of the brochures on Madison historic walking tours.

My gratitude also to Dick Burnell, East Towne Mall Walkers Club; Joe Halasz, Marquette Trail; Maxine Thoorsell, Duck Lake Nature Trail; Nathan Seppa, environmental reporter for the *Wisconsin State Journal;* and Alex Kailing of the Wisconsin Society for Ornithology.

The many rough spots in my copy were very professionally smoothed out by University of Wisconsin Press editor-in-chief Elizabeth Steinberg, editor Carol Olsen, and copy editor Diana

Cook. Thanks also to the Cartographic Laboratory of the University of Wisconsin–Madison and director Onno Brouwer, for preparing the handsome maps.

I, and all who use the trails described in this guide, owe a special thank you to the workers—many of whom are volunteers—who built and maintain them. They are not only from state, county, and city agencies, but also from such organizations as the Ice Age Park & Trail Foundation, The Nature Conservancy, the Audubon Society, the Friends of the University of Wisconsin Arboretum, the Wisconsin Society for Ornithology, the Sierra Club, and other groups who work behind the scenes to make our walking experiences so pleasurable.

Introduction

A few years ago while getting a physical examination I complained to the doctor that sometimes an elbow or knee would hurt or feel stiff in the morning when I got out of bed. "Your joints just start getting a little rusty when you get into middle age," he said. I couldn't fault him for clouding his explanation with arcane medical jargon.

One of several reasons I started walking at least a half-hour a day was to delay the onset of "rust," and it has helped. But I've become captivated by unexpected fringe benefits of walking—the mental and emotional aspects of it. If you're like me, you'll find that as you start your walk, your body invites your mind to assume a new attitude.

For me the effect is different on different days, depending on whether I'm involved in a difficult activity or problem when I start my walk, or the time of day I go, or whether I'm alone or with a companion, or often where I choose to walk. That walking can relieve emotional pressure is well known. Stress seems to steadily evaporate as the body gets into the rhythm of this low-key exercise.

But it gets even better. My thinking becomes better organized, probably because walking separates me from the distractions of the place I start from. The slower pace of walking, as opposed to riding in a car, helps me to become more observant of the details of my surroundings. When walking in a place I haven't visited recently it's great to simply enjoy the sense of discovery I feel. On some days, when walking alone on a little-used trail, I find that just the solitude is rewarding.

I've tried to describe enough of a variety of places in this book to offer you a similarly wide range of walking experiences. The book isn't an exhaustive list of trails in southern Wisconsin, and I'm sure it doesn't even include all the best ones. I hope you'll tell me about your favorite places if you don't find them here so we may both share them with others in the next edition. Please write to me at this address: Bob Crawford, 1864 Barrington Dr., Sun Prairie, WI 53590. Use a photocopy of the form printed on the last page of this book.

Writing this guide and going through the many necessary

steps of publishing have taken a lot longer than I originally thought they would. So while I've made a sincere attempt to make sure all trail descriptions are up-to-date, things will change. If you've discovered that parts of my trail descriptions are significantly out-of-date, please drop me a line at the address above.

The rating system

I've rated the difficulty of each trail or walking place from one to five, as illustrated by the number of shoes. Lower numbers indicate easier walking. While I've walked at least partway in every place described in these pages, I haven't walked the entire length of all trails, or every trail within a place that has several trails. And I obviously haven't been to all locations in all seasons of the year. So I readily admit that the system is highly subjective.

In general, I've tried to gauge the difficulty of each place by taking into account the amount of grade or slope, paving or lack of it, width, possible muddiness or slipperiness in wet weather, clarity of signs or markings, and general maintenance. I think you'll find my ratings to be conservative. An especially physically fit walker will experience less difficulty on many trails than my ratings imply. I've attempted to gauge difficulty for the hiker of average endurance, like myself. While the system is far from perfect, I hope it helps you decide at least to some degree when and where to take your walks and what to expect there.

You will notice that trail descriptions in this book are grouped by county. Each county section begins with a map of the county containing key numbers indicating the location of trails described in that section. However, some trails cross county boundaries. Each inter-county trail is described in one county section and is also located by a key letter on the maps of other counties that it crosses.

Walking Trails of Southern Wisconsin

Columbia County

Give me the clear blue sky over my head, and the green turf beneath my feet, a winding road before me, and a three-hours' march to dinner—and then to thinking!

William Hazlitt, On Going a Journey

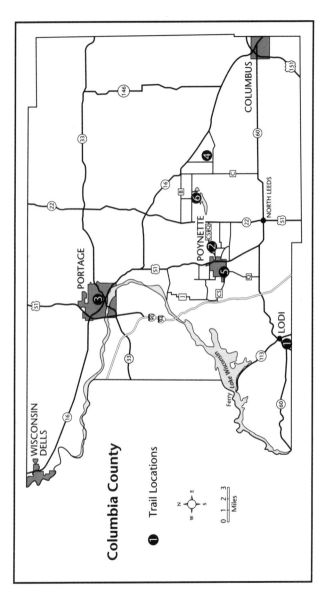

Columbia County

● Trail Locations

N
W — E
S

0 1 2 3
Miles

1 Climb a Ridge for Dramatic Views of Lodi Marsh

Lodi Marsh Segment, Ice Age National Scenic Trail, Lodi

When the Laurentide Ice Sheet moved through southern Wisconsin, south of Lodi it moved east to west over the tops of high ridges and gouged out a basin for what is now a diverse wetland known as Lodi Marsh.

Climbing some 250 feet in a half-mile to the top of one of those ridges, a segment of the Ice Age National Scenic Trail provides several dramatic scenic overlooks of the marsh and surrounding hills. From Dave's View at the top of the ridge, you can see the Baraboo Hills on the northern horizon and get a sweeping view of hills and valleys nearly to Sauk City to the west.

Description and special features. The 3.5-mile trail goes roughly northeast to southwest along the ridge. The steep half-mile climb is at the northeast end. Toward the southwest the trail descends into a valley, climbs the other side partway up a hill, and runs along the side of the hill before it descends again. After crossing Lodi-Springfield Road it goes into lowlands bordering the marsh, through an oak savanna, and out over a prairie near the foot of Center Bluff.

For convenience, I recommend you start your hike from a parking lot off Lodi-Springfield Road where the trail crosses the road. This portion of the trail is closer to the best views.

After parking your car, cross the road and begin your walk up the gentle slope and across the side of the hill. You'll get the best view of the marsh after you reach the valley and climb to what appears to be an old agricultural road on the other side of it. The basin for the marsh was most likely formed by a slab of ice that was "hung up" there as the glacier receded, according to Gary Werner of the Ice Age Park and Trail Foundation, Inc. He points out that although the glacier formed this basin traveling east to west, Spring Creek, which now meanders through it, flows northeast.

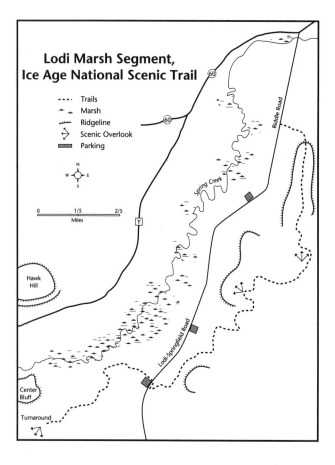

Lodi Marsh Segment, Ice Age National Scenic Trail

Trails
Marsh
Ridgeline
Scenic Overlook
Parking

N
W   E
S

0   1/5   2/5
Miles

60

60

Y

Riddle Road

Spring Creek

Lodi-Springfield Road

Hawk Hill

Center Bluff

Turnaround

Look west down the valley into the marsh. The lush wetland is bracketed by Center Bluff on the left and Hawk Hill, where The Nature Conservancy has a preserve, on the right.

Continue your climb up the main ridge through mixed evergreens and hardwoods to a prairie at the top called Dave's View, which was named for one of the original trail workers. From this vantage point your view will take in some 50 square miles of hill and valley landscape formed by the glacier.

On the other side of the prairie you'll cross a lane clear cut for power transmission lines, re-enter the woods, and begin a steep descent to the northeast end of the trail. If you're too tired to climb back up the hill, you can return to the parking lot by the road, a walk of about 1.5 miles.

The lowlands portion of the trail, a shorter segment, goes west from the parking lot over a prairie and a low hill bordering the marsh. Trail builders have gotten help from Boy Scouts to cut underbrush and small trees and restore an oak savanna on a knoll next to the marsh. The trail ends at an overlook near Center Bluff.

Degree of difficulty. The unpaved trail is wide, except for the northeast one-half mile, and well marked. I first walked it in winter when it was covered with about three inches of snow. Although the trail ascends some steep grades, I had difficulty with footing only on the steeper northeast portion.

How to get there. From State Highway 60 just south of Lodi, go south on Riddle Road, which becomes Lodi-Springfield Road as it crosses the border from Columbia to Dane County, for two miles to the above-mentioned parking lot on the right.

If you wish to begin at the northeast end of the trail, go south on Riddle Road from Highway 60 one-half mile to the trail entrance on the left. The trailhead sign is slightly off the road and easy to miss, and you cannot park along the road without blocking a gate to a farm field. You will find a parking lot on the right another 0.4 mile south.

When open. The year around. The trail runs through the Lodi Marsh State Wildlife Area, which is open to hunters during spring and fall seasons. Wear bright clothing during these times.

Cross-country skiers may also use the trail when snow conditions permit.

Facilities. The most convenient parking lot is located at the point where the trail crosses Lodi-Springfield Road.

Other points of interest in area

Lodi, north of the trail on State Highways 60 and 113, is a scenic town of some 2,000 citizens. It has three city parks, a nine-hole golf course, and a giant swimming pool. Spring Creek, which flows from Lodi Marsh through the village, is home of Susie the Duck and her mallard descendants, who have nested near a bridge on Main Street since 1948.

2 Discover Forestry and Wildlife Secrets on Six Trails

MacKenzie Environmental Education Center, Poynette

👟

Learn about ecology, forestry, and local flora and fauna on the well-maintained trails of this center, which has evolved in a way different from the average state park.

Description and special features. "Environmental education is our purpose for being here," says Derek Duane, director of the center. "There's some confusion about us. We're not a state park, so we don't charge a user fee." Duane explains that the Bureau of Information and Education of the Department of Natural Resources (DNR) operates the center, while another DNR division runs the state parks. "As our mission statement says, our purpose is to provide environmental education opportunities for youths and adults so they may appreciate and understand Wisconsin's natural resources . . . to act as environmentally aware, responsible and committed citizens," Duane says.

About 50,000 people use the center each year. They come mostly from Wisconsin, but also from surrounding states and foreign countries. "We had one group from the Republic of Tatar" (in the former Soviet Union), Duane said. "We were cautioned that they didn't like to be called Russians."

Each of six trails has its own printed self-guide, which is available at the beginning of the trail. Before starting your walks, stop at the headquarters office to obtain a tabloid brochure with background information and map of the entire center. Designers made sure all trails are loops that begin and end in a parking lot. Trails are as follows:

Wildlife Trail. This is actually two trails in one, with the shorter portion paved. The full trail is one-half mile in length. Eight informational stops tell how to build feeders, nesting boxes, and cover for wildlife, and provide other ways to promote the propagation of small animals on your own property.

9

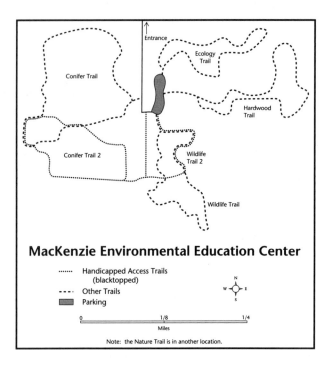

MacKenzie Environmental Education Center

- ······· Handicapped Access Trails (blacktopped)
- ----· Other Trails
- ▨ Parking

0   1/8   1/4
Miles

Note: the Nature Trail is in another location.

Conifer Trail and Conifer Trail 2. These two trails intersect and have a total of 29 informational stops that identify various species of conifer and provide other information about the nature of conifer forests. Conifer 2 is level and fully paved with side bumper rail. The trails are roughly equal in length at about 0.4 mile each.

Hardwood Trail. This somewhat hilly trail goes about one-half mile through a deciduous forest. The 18 stops provide forestry information for the production of quality lumber.

Ecology Trail. The plant and animal ecosystem of an oak forest is described and explained in the 14 informational stations of this short trail. Signs identify the four types of oak in the forest: white, red, bur, and black.

Nature Trail. You may enter this trail at many points along the way. The trail includes a fire tower, which you may climb to the 40-foot level. Live white-tailed deer, bison, and a wildlife pond are among the exhibits. You may also tour a logging museum and an "aliens" (non-native plants and animals) museum on the trail. This varied trail also has an example of a huge, 250-year-old pine log, from a tree that was common in Wisconsin's northern forests before initial logging.

Degree of difficulty. Two trails are accessible to strollers, wheelchairs, and others with limited mobility. Conifer Trail 2 is level and fully paved, while Wildlife Trail is paved partway. Other trails are sand or gravel with varying small slopes, but none is difficult to walk. All trails are very well maintained. Distance for all trails totals 3.5 miles.

How to get there. From U.S. Hwy. 51 in Poynette, go east on County Q and CS for 2 miles to the MacKenzie entrance on the right. First, you will come to the office, arboretum, and nature trail. Drive about one-quarter mile south for other trails.

When open. You may walk the trails any day of the year, but they are not plowed or maintained in winter. The office and museums are open from dawn to dusk every day from the first week in May to mid-October. The rest of the year, they are open Monday through Friday except on holidays.

Facilities. The center has a large picnic area. Flush toilets (handicap accessible) are available at the picnic area until cold weather comes (there are pit toilets for winter use) and in the lower level of the main office building.

Groups may use a resident center with bunks, showers, and a kitchen for $4 per day per person with a $100 minimum. Overnight and day-use groups must make reservations in advance (telephone 608 635-4498). Individuals cannot be accommodated overnight, but they may use the center at any time without registering.

Other points of interest in area

Two important bird sanctuaries are nearby, both owned by the Madison, Wisconsin, Audubon Society. Goose Pond Sanctuary is located southeast of Poynette in an open prairie. From the town of Leeds on U.S. 51, go west on County K for about two miles, then north on Goose Pond Road to Prairie Lane. A prairie hiking trail is across the road from the pond. The Society recently purchased 80 acres of Otsego Marsh, east of Poynette, which includes a primitive woodland and marsh hiking trail. (See pp. 17–18.)

You'll enjoy an excellent marsh-walking experience at Rowan Creek Trail, which begins on the west edge of Poynette at the end of Mill Street. (See pp. 19–22.)

See a modern milking parlor at the University of Wisconsin Experimental Farms between 2 and 4 P.M. daily. Go south on Goose Pond Road, east on County K, and north on Hopkins Road. The milking parlor is just east of the Agronomy and Headquarters buildings.

3 Trace the Footsteps of Père Marquette and Joliet

Marquette Trail, Portage

The history of the exploration and settlement of not only Wisconsin but the nation is tied to this area. The Fox-Wisconsin portage (which follows Wauona Trail on your walk) was the only bridge of land on this major water route through the midcontinent between the Atlantic Ocean and the Gulf of Mexico. Jesuit missionary Father Marquette and explorer Louis Joliet, the first white men to make the portage, and their guides and companions paddled from Green Bay up the Fox River in 1673. Crossing on foot to the Wisconsin, Marquette wrote, "We now leave the waters that flow to Quebec to follow those which henceforth lead us to strange lands."

Description. From the parking lot take a footbridge across the Fox-Wisconsin canal and follow a footpath for about three-fourths mile. The path, which is also part of the Ice Age National Scenic Trail, was built mostly atop a ridge of fill dredged to form the canal in the nineteenth century.

Upon reaching State Highway 33 go to the right across the bridge and follow the dirt road to the left next to the canal about one-third mile to its end. Cross the railroad tracks. (These tracks are part of the Amtrak route between Chicago and Minneapolis–St. Paul.)

Pick up the footpath on the other side. It leads to Edgewater Street, which you'll follow nearly a mile to DeWitt Street in downtown Portage. Turn left, cross the canal again and, on the other side, turn right at Mullet Street. Follow Mullet to its end, through a parking lot, and into a small park next to the Wisconsin River locks.

From the locks walk east atop the Wisconsin River levee about a mile. For the latter portion of the mile the levee borders East Wisconsin Street. At the corner of East Wisconsin and Wauona Trail, a street to the left, you'll see a monument dedicated to Marquette and Joliet. Take Wauona Trail 1.3 miles, turn right and follow State Highway 33 for about 0.5 mile across the

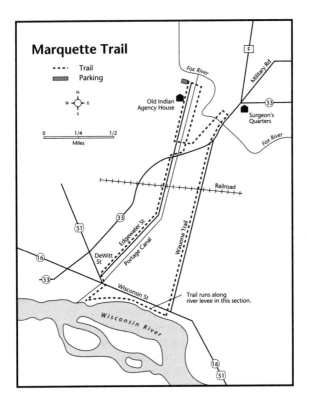

Marquette Trail

- - - - Trail
▬▬▬ Parking

N
W ✦ E
S

0   1/4   1/2
Miles

Fox River

Old Indian
Agency House

F

Military Rd

33

Surgeon's
Quarters

Fox River

Railroad

33

51

Edgewater St

Portage Canal

Wauona Trail

16

33

DeWitt
St

Wisconsin St

Trail runs along
river levee in this section.

Wisconsin River

16

51

Fox River bridge. On the right is the old Surgeon's Quarters and on the left a wayside park containing several monuments.

Retrace your steps along Highway 33 to the canal, cross the bridge, and go right on Agency House Road to the Old Indian Agency House and the parking lot beyond.

For exceptionally ambitious and sure-footed hikers, the Ice Age National Scenic Trail continues from the parking lot north along the banks of the Fox another 7 miles to Governor's Bend Park. Be prepared to cross streams on old footbridges made of telephone poles on this sporadically maintained portion of the trail.

Special features. Like the Panama Canal, the Portage Canal took many years to complete, with at least one failed attempt along the way. It was opened in 1876, and the first river steamer traveled through locks that dropped the water level an average of eight feet from the Wisconsin to the Fox. However, with the coming of the railroad, traffic through the canal never reached expected levels. The locks were closed in 1951.

Begun in 1882 and built to prevent frequent flooding of the area, the Wisconsin River Levee you hike extends 17 miles on both sides of the river. From atop the levee you view the east channel of the river, which is separated from the west channel by a mile-long island at this location.

A red granite marker at the west end of Wauona Trail where Marquette and Joliet put their canoes into the Wisconsin commemorates their journey across the portage. You travel the portage along Wauona Trail opposite the direction they did. They lifted their canoes from the Fox near the location of the wayside park on State Highway 33. A monument in the park marks the site of Fort Winnebago, which was built in 1828 to secure the portage and protect area settlers from Indian attacks. Lt. Jefferson Davis, later president of the Confederacy, helped build the fort. Fire destroyed the fort in 1856.

Only the Surgeon's Quarters, a home adjacent to the fort, remains. The government purchased it from pioneer François LeRoi to house army doctors stationed at the fort. Restored and refurnished as a typical pioneer house, it is open 10 A.M. to 4 P.M. daily from May 15 through October 15. Admission is charged.

Across the river from the wayside park, a monument commemorates Pierre Pauquette, a colorful pioneer character of Indian and French lineage who, among other things, operated a ferry across the Wisconsin. Pauquette was murdered by an Indian who mistakenly thought the burly pioneer betrayed him.

Completed in 1832 for the Indian agent John Kinzie and his wife, Juliette, the Old Indian Agency House served as a trading and social center for whites and Indians. Mrs. Kinzie chronicled activities at the house and the fort in her book, *Wau-bun*. You may tour the house, which is full of authentic furniture from the early 1800s, from 10 A.M. to 4 P.M. the year around (off-season by appointment). The National Society of Colonial Dames in Wisconsin charges a small admission.

Degree of difficulty. Easy on mostly paved streets or sidewalks for the 6-mile itinerary described here.

How to get there. From I-90–94 take the Portage exit at State Highway 78 from the south or State Highway 33 from the north. From Highway 78, go east on Highway 33, through town, to the Agency House Road just before the Portage Canal bridge. Turn left and go about three-fourths mile to the parking lot at end of road.

Facilities. Parking at the trailhead.

Other points of interest in area

One-quarter mile northeast of the fort site on County EE, Fort Winnebago Cemetery contains graves of soldiers stationed at the fort. At least one fought in the revolutionary war.

At the Zona Gale Home, 506 West Edgewater Street, you can see where the winner of the 1921 Pulitzer Prize in Drama for her play *Miss Lulu Bett* grew up and wrote. Now owned by the Portage Women's Civic League, the home has a classic Greek Revival exterior that contrasts dramatically with other homes along the Wisconsin River banks. You may tour it for a small fee by appointment (telephone 608 742-7744).

4 Quiet Trail Borders Audubon Society's Pond

Otsego Marsh Trail, southern Columbia County

When southern Columbia and northern Dane counties were settled, lush prairies created one of the most productive farming areas in the state. Well into the twentieth century, as farmers sought to put still more land under the plow, wetlands were considered wastelands with no economic value. Many were drained without considering the consequences for wildlife, believed to be in endless supply. The objective, horizon-to-horizon farming, was considered the best use of the land.

But some wetlands were saved. Otsego Marsh with its goose pond was probably just a little too deep to be drained. Escaping the trench digger, the 80-acre site is now one of the choicest bird-watching locations in the area. The Madison Audubon Society recently acquired the site, with the help of The Nature Conservancy.

From the looping trail during my summer walk there, I saw pairs of sandhill cranes and large white egrets. Migrating Canada geese also flock to the pond in the spring and fall, and mallards stay all summer.

Description and special features. Two trailheads begin on the east side of Old F. The one on the right goes into a thick pine plantation and loops back to the main trail. I suggest taking the left trail, which follows the southern border of the pond and offers the best chance to see the big birds.

After going straight east for several hundred yards, you'll reach a fork that is the base of a loop. Go left to continue along the pond. The trail then veers right, circles through a large, mature stand of hardwoods, and returns to the base of the loop. Total distance including the trail through the conifer plantation is about 1.5 miles.

Degree of difficulty. Though it goes over mostly flat or gently sloped terrain, the trail is primitive and narrow. Thick undergrowth can make going difficult in midsummer and a carpet of leaves obscures the path in the fall. The immature foliage of spring allows the most unobstructed view of the pond. Bright yellow markers on steel posts will keep you on track.

How to get there. From State Highway 22 in southern Columbia County, go east on King Road 5.3 miles to Old F, turn left and go .2 mile. The trail is on the right.

When open. You may walk this little-used trail the year around.

Facilities. Park along the road. Along the trail are several benches for resting and wildlife viewing and two picnic tables, though this seems to be an unlikely location for leisurely lunching. Bring your bug spray and pack out your trash.

Other points of interest in area

Another important bird sanctuary nearby, also owned by the Madison Audubon Society, is Goose Pond Sanctuary. From the town of Leeds on U.S. 51, go west on County K for about 2 miles to Goose Pond Road, then right to Prairie Lane. A prairie hiking trail is across the road from the pond.

You'll enjoy an excellent marsh-walking experience at Rowan Creek Trail. The trail begins on the west edge of Poynette at the end of Mill Street. (See pp. 19–22.)

See a modern milking parlor at the University of Wisconsin Experimental Farms between 2 and 4 P.M. daily. Go south on Goose Pond Road, turn east on County K and south on Hopkins Road. The milking parlor is just east of the Agronomy and Headquarters buildings.

5 Walk the Wetlands but Keep Your Feet Dry

Rowan Creek Trail, Poynette

👟 👟

Developed and maintained by the Wisconsin Department of Natural Resources and opened in late 1989, Rowan Creek Trail is ideal for walking, observing wildlife, and cross-country skiing. It is one of the best constructed wetland trails I've walked. Your feet will stay dry while you experience a variety of wetland features: the gently flowing stream, spikey cattail marshes, and twig-carpeted bottomland. The itinerary also includes several kinds of upland forests of hardwoods and conifers.

Description and special features. To the right of the Mill Street parking lot near the head of the trail are the remnants of the Poynette Millpond Dam. Only abutments remain of a concrete structure that was about 10 feet high and 2 feet thick at the bottom. It was built in 1860, breached in 1940 to drain the pond, and largely removed in 1987 to allow the creek to run free.

From the Mill Street entrance, always take the right branch of any loop coming and going to travel the entire trail. The trail begins alongside Rowan Creek and follows the gently flowing trout stream for a fraction of a mile. Anglers catch brown trout just a few feet from the trail. (See Department of Natural Resources regulations.)

Leaving the creek, the trail snakes through a hardwood forest and several cattail marshes. You'll cross the marshes with ease via wide, well-made boardwalks. DNR staff bolted them to foam-filled plastic culverts that serve as floating pontoons when the water level is high. There are 750 feet of these marvels of wetland construction. "We built one of these and tested it in a water tank before constructing them for the trail," Tim Larson, DNR trail supervisor, told me.

The trail culminates in a loop on Pine Island, through a stand of tall conifers planted in 1930.

You'll have many chances to see wildlife on this trail. Skirting or traversing wetlands much of the way, you may see white-tail

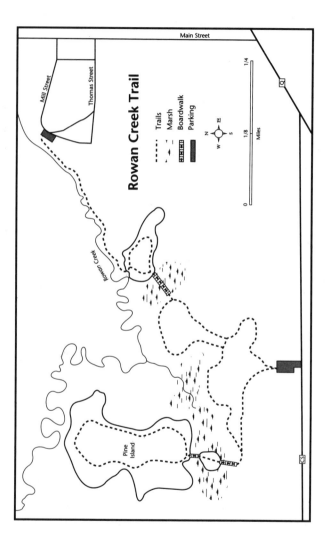

Rowan Creek Trail

Trails
Marsh
Boardwalk
Parking

Main Street

Mill Street

Thomas Street

Rowan Creek

Pine Island

N
W · E
S

0   1/8   1/4
Miles

deer standing in your path, raccoons waddling across the trail, mallards or wood ducks plying the marsh ponds.

Box turtles splash as you pass and bullfrogs sing their throaty songs in the marshes. My wife and I saw or heard over a dozen kinds of birds, including a great blue heron that flushed and flew away noisily, probably to distract us from its nest, during our walk. In spring wildflowers—marsh marigolds and hepatica—decorate the banks of the creek. With the many maples, aspens, oaks, and red sumac along the trail, an autumn walk also is an adventure of color.

Degree of difficulty. The trail is approximately 3.5 miles round trip, including several alternative loops. Wide and with only a few small hills, the trail is easy for those in good health. Wood chips cover sections that might be muddy during wet weather. Wide bridges or boardwalks span wetlands. Stop and relax during your walk on any of seven sturdy wood benches.

How to get there. Exit I-90–94 at Poynette and either (1) travel east on County CS for several miles to a parking lot on the left, or (2) continue on CS to Main Street in Poynette, go north on Main Street, turn left at the Methodist church onto Mill Street, and park in the lot near the end of Mill Street and the trailhead. Of the two entrances, I prefer the latter.

When open. The year around.

Facilities. Parking at the trailheads.

Other points of interest in area

Two miles east of Poynette on County CS, the MacKenzie Environmental Education Center is another paradise for walkers (see chapter 1.2). Open dawn to dusk the year around except during deer hunting season, the center has six self-guided nature trails, live native wildlife exhibits, fire tower, and museums featuring conservation and non-native plants and animals. Also see a sawmill, a wildlife pond, and an arboretum with over 100 kinds of trees and shrubs. You could easily spend an entire day walking the trails and viewing exhibits.

Lake Wisconsin, about 6 miles west of Poynette on County

CS, was formed in the 1920s by the construction of Prairie du Sac hydroelectric dam. This 9,000-acre lake provides excellent boating and water skiing. Fishing, especially for northern and walleye pike and bass, is said to be very good. It's also okay to swim, though there are few good beaches, and the water, fed by the Wisconsin River, is not the clearest.

Jamieson House, an elegantly restored Victorian mansion located north of downtown near Main Street, was the residence of Poynette's founder, Hugh Jamieson. It is now a bed and breakfast inn.

6 Trail Penetrates Area Teeming with Wildlife

Mud Lake State Wildlife Area, Rio

👟 👟 👟 👟

A 1,900-acre area that is a favorite of hunters, fishermen, and bird watchers centers on Mud Lake, which is shallow, marshy, and big. It literally teems with wild things that inhabit it the year-around, and it's a regular stop over for migrating waterfowl and other birds. Not many hikers have discovered the delightful trail that penetrates right into the middle of the wildlife area.

Description and special features. Starting from a small parking lot off Tollefson Road, the trail follows the fringe of a hardwood forest and then enters it. Several small, placid ponds occupy potholes on either side of the trail. During a springtime walk I saw a half-dozen greater scaups, members of the duck family whose summer range is nearer the Arctic Circle, plying one of them. The male scaup is adorned in deep black, bright white, and light greenish grey.

Take the right branch of a fork in the trail to continue among the potholes,and you'll eventually emerge from the woods onto a meadow. The trail leads to a causeway that divides the marsh. If you don't see sandhill cranes from this area, especially in the spring, you will very likely hear their throaty call.The Audubon Society also reports sightings of moorhens and black-crowned night herons in the marsh, in addition to a variety of ducks and large flocks of Canada geese.

Across the causeway the trail veers to the left and up a low hill that was once under plow. This portion of the trail is not maintained and may be overgrown. The view from the top of the hill takes in most of Mud Lake and surrounding marshes.

Degree of difficulty. Following gently rolling or level terrain, the trail is wide but unpaved. It is not cleared in winter.

How to get there. From North Leeds, take State Highway 22 north for 6.5miles to Drake Road, go right (east) 2.7 miles to Tollefson Road on the right. (Tollefson Road is not marked, but a large sign denotes Mud Lake Wildlife Area.) Take Tollefson a fraction of a mile around a bend to the right and halfway up a hill. You'll find a small parking lot on the left at the gated trailhead.

When open. The year around. Hunters also roam the area during their seasons. Wear bright clothing, especially in the spring and fall.

Facilities. Parking.

Dane County

I think that I cannot preserve my health and spirits, unless I spend four hours a day at least,—and it's commonly more than that,—sauntering through the woods and over the hills and fields, absolutely free from all worldly engagements.

Henry David Thoreau, WALKING

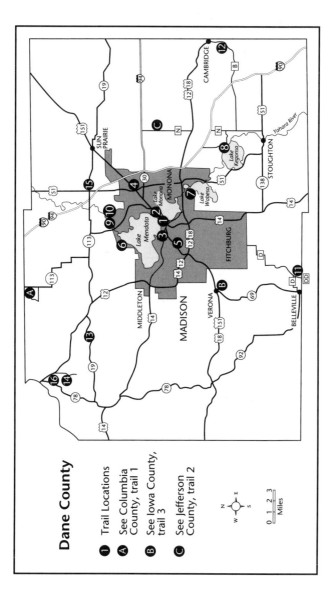

Dane County

- **1** Trail Locations
- **A** See Columbia County, trail 1
- **B** See Iowa County, trail 3
- **C** See Jefferson County, trail 2

N
W E
S

0 1 2 3
Miles

26

1 From the Capitol Square to the Best Campus View

Capitol Square and Near West Side, Madison

👟 👟

This walk has something for everyone. As you exercise, you'll experience one of the more beautiful capitol buildings in the nation, dozens of specialty shops, a breathtaking view of the city's largest lake, and people-watching of great variety.

Description and special features. From the junction of Mifflin Street and State Street, start walking south on Carroll Street and follow the Square around the capitol until you return to the junction. Then go west on State Street to the base of the University of Wisconsin campus at Park Street. Follow the students up Bascom Hill, to the right around Bascom Hall, and along the sidewalk bordering Observatory Drive to the top of the hill. Return east along Observatory Drive to Langdon Street. Follow Langdon to Wisconsin Avenue, and Wisconsin south to the Square.

The Capitol Square–State Street portion of this itinerary is probably the most popular route for casual walkers in Madison. Of course, a highlight of the walk is the State Capitol. Among capitol buildings in the United States it is second in height only to the national capitol in Washington, D.C. Completed in 1917, this magnificent structure contains marble and granite from throughout the world, as well as distinguished historical paintings and statuary. It houses all three branches of state government: legislative, judicial, and executive. Plan to spend an hour touring its many halls and chambers. Free tours are conducted on the hour from 9 A.M. to 3 P.M. Monday through Saturday and at 1, 2, and 3 P.M. Sunday.

On the second floor of the State Historical Society Museum at 30 North Carroll Street is a permanent exhibit of Woodland Indian life from prehistoric times to the present. Temporary exhibits on the first floor change three or four times per year. In the museum shop, you'll find books about not just Wisconsin history but genealogy, travel, art, cooking, and a host of other subjects with a Wisconsin theme. Exhibits are free. The museum is open 10 A.M. to 5 P.M. Tuesday through Saturday, closed major holidays.

The Madison Civic Center, 211 State Street, is the result of a detailed renovation of the Capitol Theater, a 1920s movie house with a fanciful Moorish interior, and rebuilding of adjoining structures. Designed by architects Hardy Holzman Pfeiffer Associates, it was completed in 1980. The Hispano-Moorish exterior of the theater was retained with only minor enhancement. The interior, however, is a celebration of 1920s period design.

In the Civic Center, the Madison Art Center sponsors exhibits of local or national significance that change every few weeks and may be viewed for a few dollars or less. The four-level Crossroads (lobby) opens at 7:30 A.M. and closes at 5:30 P.M., later on evenings of performances. It's not unusual for a free concert to be offered over the lunch hour.

While commercial outdoor pedestrian malls are declining elsewhere, the six or so blocks of State Street are a parade of activity. Gift shops, clothing (new and used) stores, restaurants and coffee shops, taverns and specialty shops face the mall. Spend some time browsing to enjoy State Street to its fullest.

The University of Wisconsin–Madison campus borders Park Street at the west end of State Street. The walk up the path along Observatory Drive overlooking Lake Mendota provides a startlingly beautiful lake view.

Enjoy watching students along Langdon Street's Fraternity Row. Fraternity and sorority houses and other buildings, many built during the 1910s and 1920s, exemplify a wide variety of architectures. On Langdon and adjoining side streets you'll see Colonial and Georgian revival, Mediterranean and Tudor revival, and other old architectural forms revived with the help of ample alumni subsidies. A few historical homes of Madison pioneers also remain on Langdon Street.

Degree of difficulty. It's an easy to moderate 3.4-mile walk on sidewalks with only a few busy crosswalks on State Street. The campus portion of the walk is hilly, but not too strenuous.

How to get there. From U.S. 12 and 18 (the Beltline), take John Nolen Drive northwest to downtown Madison. Park in the

Capitol Centre parking ramp on Mifflin Street two blocks west of the Capitol Square. It is lowest in cost and nearly always has space available. Walk east to the Square on Mifflin Street.

Facilities. Rest rooms are available in the capitol.

2 Brochures Describe Eight Historical Tours in "City of Lakes"

Neighborhood Walking Tours, Madison

It has gracefully rolling hills. It has three beautiful lakes. It has a rich history. No wonder the city of Madison in south central Wisconsin is an unusually interesting and pleasant place to walk. At the urging of Alderperson Henry Lufler and mayoral staffer Anne Monks, the Madison Landmarks Commission publishes a continuing series of walking tour brochures that describe the history of neighborhoods, their old buildings, and other important historical sites. Each brochure has an easy-to-follow map.

Brochures described nine tours at this writing, and more are on the way as funding allows, according to commission staffer and brochure editor Katherine Rankin. The city, the Dane County Cultural Affairs Commission, and several corporations and individuals provide monies.

Description and special features. Brochures have been published or soon will be for the following tours. You will find free copies at the main public library, 201 West Mifflin Street, and its branches. Because of a brisk demand for them and a limited budget, some brochures are not always available for free distribution, but most may be borrowed by library cardholders. Copies may also be available at room GR100 in the Municipal Building, 215 Martin Luther King, Jr., Boulevard.

The Langdon Street Historic District. Northwest of the capitol and east of the University of Wisconsin along Lake Mendota, the whole district has been listed on the National Register of Historic Places. Starting in the latter half of the nineteenth century prominent citizens built homes of impressive size and noteworthy architecture. Many of the homes now house fraternities or sororities.

Madison's Pioneer Buildings. With a population of 626, Madison became an incorporated village in 1846. An explosion of growth followed as Wisconsin became the thirtieth state in 1848. The new legislature selected the capital city as the site of the state university. This walking tour features homes, commercial buildings, and churches, many of which were built between 1850 and 1880.

The First Settlement Neighborhood. This tour of the near east side from the Capitol Square to Lake Monona includes older homes and commercial buildings, two churches, a railroad depot, and a meeting hall.

The Third Lake Ridge Historic District. Retailing, manufacturing, and residences form the diverse character of this district. The ridge, along the northern rim of Lake Monona, is actually a long drumlin, a landform created by the continental glacier. Houses exemplify a variety of architectural styles.

Schenk's-Atwood Neighborhood. Farther along Lake Monona and east of the Yahara River another commercial-residential neighborhood developed. Highlights of this tour include manufacturing plants, churches, and homes. Perhaps 1,000 years ago Woodland Indians built effigy mounds, believed to be of a bear and a lynx, near the lakeshore.

University Heights Historic District. Its location just west of the growing University of Wisconsin campus ensured that this neighborhood, developed between 1893 and 1941, would be home to many university faculty members and administrators. The builders of homes chose a variety of architectures. Your walking tour will reveal excellent examples of Prairie School architecture, including a home designed by Frank Lloyd Wright. You'll also see examples of Georgian Revival, Queen Anne, Tudor, Craftsman, and bungalow architecture.

Greenbush-Vilas Neighborhood. This brochure actually describes two walking tours, each with its own map. The Brittingham-Greenbush-Bayview tour along Monona Bay and west goes through the remaining portions of what was once an Italian and Jewish ethnic neighborhood known as Greenbush.

A little farther west, bordered by Vilas Park on the south, a tour through the Wingra Park–Oakland Heights neighborhood is highlighted by moderately priced homes of late nineteenth- and early twentieth-century vintage. When walking this neighborhood, be sure also to tour Vilas Park and its fine free zoo.

Old Market Place Neighborhood. This newest of the eight brochures describes landmark homes and other buildings in the neighborhood bordered by Webster and Hamilton streets on the west, East Washington Avenue on the south, North Brearly Street on the east and Lake Mendota on the north. The area gets its name from a farmers' marketplace called City Market that was built near its center in 1909.

Architect-designed homes of early mayors and other prominent citizens still stand among those on the moraine bordering Lake Mendota. Lincoln School and Madison Water Works, both now converted into stylish apartments, also grace the neighborhood, which was originally settled in the 1850s.

Dudgeon-Monroe Neighborhood. The only brochure of the series not originated by the Madison Landmarks Commission describes a walking and biking tour centered on Monroe Street and side streets. The commission has financed brochure reprinting.

Degree of difficulty. You'll follow these tours mostly in neighborhoods with well-maintained sidewalks.

How to get there. Madison is in south central Wisconsin just west of the junction of I-90–94.

3 Follow in the Footsteps of Giants—Past and Future

University of Wisconsin Campus, Madison

When walking the streets and byways of the university, you follow in the footsteps of giants—Nobel Prize winners, noted scientists, authors, and artists. But you'll become increasingly aware as you dodge and swerve among some of the campus's 43,000 students between classes that you're also walking among the state's and nation's future leaders, now rushing to get to that lecture or lab section to absorb as much wisdom as possible during a short but hectic exposure to higher learning.

Description and special features. Situated on moraines and ancient lakebeds along the southwestern shore of eight-mile-wide Lake Mendota, the campus is a walker's wonderland, especially for the panoramic views of the lake. Nearly 200 campus buildings will spice your tour with their varied architecture and history. The university has published three tour guides encompassing the three major campus subdivisions. For conducted tours of the campus, inquire at the information desk on the second floor at the Memorial Union, northeast corner of Langdon and Park streets (telephone 608-262-2511).

Bascom Hill and Lower Campus. Starting at the Memorial Union on Langdon Street, this tour takes you up Bascom Hill past Helen C. White Hall, the historic Science Hall and Radio Hall, and by North Hall, once the dormitory of naturalist John Muir. Bascom Hall, traditionally the main building of the university, perches atop the hill. In front of the building, the statue of a seated Lincoln has long been a landmark.

Looping back down the hill, the tour juts over to the Elvehjem Museum of Art, named for a former university president, past the Memorial Library and back to the Union.

Henry Mall and West Campus. The longest of the three mapped tours, about two miles, begins at Elizabeth Waters Hall, a women's dormitory built in 1940. You'll enjoy an unparalleled view of the lake from Observatory Hill, site of the Washburn Observatory built in 1878 and now used for instruction.

Near the observatory on the hilltop are two Indian effigy mounds, a bird and a rare two-tailed turtle. The tour passes residence halls Slichter, Adams, and Tripp, and continues on to Steenbock Memorial Library, named after Professor Harry Steenbock, whose research produced Vitamin D by irradiation of food.

After reaching the 14-story Wisconsin Alumni Research Foundation building, you will loop back through the agricultural campus and by Russell Laboratories, which houses an insect collection with more than a million specimens, mostly from Wisconsin (a fact that won't surprise residents of the state).

Continuing on to Henry Mall, you will see the Biochemistry Building, where vitamins A and B complex were discovered by Elmer V. McCollum. In the middle of the mall is the Genetics Building, where Joshua Lederberg was a faculty member in genetics when he won Wisconsin's first Nobel Prize. Lederberg worked across the mall in what is now the Agricultural Journalism building. The tour ends near Van Hise Hall, location of university executive offices.

South Campus. This brochure covers the campus along and south of University Avenue and west of Murray Street. It begins at Vilas Communication Hall, which houses the School of Journalism as well as studios for public radio and television. It continues past Chadbourne Hall, a large women's dormitory named after Paul A. Chadbourne, an early university president who ironically was opposed to coeducation.

On the tour through the engineering campus you will view a number of science and engineering buildings, including the Medical Sciences Building, where the medical school began offering a four-year curriculum in 1924. A nuclear reactor, used as a teaching and research tool, is located in the Mechanical Engineering Building on the tour. Your walk will take you through Camp Randall, an active military camp during the Civil War. It now houses a 78,000-seat stadium and the new Dave McLain Athletic Facility. You'll walk back among buildings housing computer science, geology, meteorology, psychology, and zoology. The tour returns to Park Street and Vilas Hall.

Copies of the three tour brochures are available from the Office of University Relations, 19 Bascom Hall, Madison, WI 53706.

Lakeshore Path and Picnic Point. One of the most enjoyable walks through the university campus is not described in any brochure. The Lakeshore path begins at the Hoofers' boat dock near the north end of Park Street and goes west along the lakeshore at the foot of Bascom and Observatory hills. Take it about a mile to Willow Drive, now a walking and biking path that continues along the lakeshore and University Bay. Willow Drive was named for the Russian golden willows that border each side.

You will reach the entrance to Picnic Point on the west side of the bay. A crushed stone path takes you out onto the peninsula through a mature hardwood forest of oaks, basswoods, hickories, and maples. Toward the end of the peninsula, you'll be treated to beautiful views of Lake Mendota on both sides. There are several Indian effigy mounds and a hand pump for drinking water near the point.

For variety, you can return by a trail along the west side of the peninsula, where ancient cottonwoods grow by the shore. An additional short fitness path leads to the left from inside the gate off Willow Drive. A university bus will return to your starting place for 35 cents.

Degree of difficulty. Most of your brochure-described tours will be on wide, concrete-paved sidewalks. The only difficulty, as mentioned, involves competing for walking space with thousands of students, especially between classes. The lakeshore path is natural turf and crushed rock to Willow Drive, which is blacktopped. Well-maintained crushed rock paves the main trail to Picnic Point. Branch trails are mostly unpaved.

How to get there. The campus is located on the near west side of Madison, starting about one-half mile west of the capitol building and just west of Lake Street.

When open. While the university is in session nearly the year around, it is less populated during the summer and especially during the few weeks on either side of the mid-June to mid-August summer session, making for less congested walking. The main path to Picnic Point is plowed during the winter. It is closed to visitors at 10 P.M.

Facilities. Nearly every major building has rest room facilities. Parking, however, can be problem. I suggest the Lake Street parking ramp, near the corner of Lake and State streets. You may park for free in a lot at the gate of Picnic Point. Along the trail are picnic tables, grills, drinking water, and a swimming beach.

Other points of interest in area

Babcock Hall Ice Cream Shop, at the southwest corner of Babcock and Linden drives, was well known for its great ice cream even before the *New York Times* praised it in 1986. The store offers not only a wide variety of ice cream flavors in cones, sundaes, or cartons, but also frozen yogurt and cheese. All products are made on-site in the building's demonstration dairy processing plant. The shop is open 9:30 A.M. to 6 P.M. Monday through Friday and 9:30 to noon on Saturday.

University of Wisconsin Arboretum, located about a mile from the campus, and its many walking trails are described on pp. 39–42.

4 Escape from Winter without Going to Florida

East Towne Mall, Madison

Okay, the temperature outside is minus 10, or worse yet 35 degrees and raining. You don't want to interrupt your daily walking routine, but you also don't want to catch pneumonia. Where do you go? In Madison, the mall is a good answer.

Description and special features. An entirely enclosed retail shopping mall, East Towne opens at 10 A.M. six days and 11 A.M. Sunday. Doors close at 9 P.M. Monday through Friday, 5:30 P.M. Saturday, and 5 P.M. Sunday.

If you'd rather walk earlier, consider joining the East Towne Mall Walkers Club, which has special permission from mall management to walk its spacious halls from 6 A.M. daily and 7:30 A.M. Sunday until the mall is opened to shoppers. The main door on the west side and the rear door on the east side are opened early for walkers.

The club collects no membership dues. "It's very easy to join. You just show up and start walking," says Dick Burnell, retired Air Force master sergeant and informal consensus club president. The club keeps no membership rolls, but Burnell encourages members to register with mall management and provide information that might be useful in case of a health emergency.

Optional monthly meetings usually feature health concerns with a talk by a doctor or a representative of a fitness club. Burnell, who writes a newsletter for members and maintains a portable bulletin board, also organizes occasional bus trips to such places as a dog track or gambling riverboat. When I spoke to him in November 1993, the club had 862 members.

Degree of difficulty. The complete circuit of the hallways is 0.7 mile. In mild weather some walkers circle the mall on an outside concrete walk, which measures exactly a mile, according to Burnell. The entire indoor route is on one level with no stairs.

How to get there. East Towne is on the southeast side of U.S. 151 (East Washington Avenue) about 1 mile east of U.S. 51 and 0.5 mile west of I-90–94.

Facilities. Parking, rest rooms, and plenty of areas to sit and rest. A few restaurants open early to serve coffee to walkers. The unofficial rallying point is in the food court.

Other points of interest in area

Other major indoor malls are: West Towne Mall, Gammon Road just north of the Beltline Highway; South Towne Mall, near the intersection of West Broadway and the Beltline; Westgate, on Whitney Way one block north of the Beltline; and Hilldale, on Midvale Boulevard at University Avenue.

Another excellent indoor walking place is the state capitol, on Capitol Square in downtown Madison.

5 Tour a Giant Laboratory of Restored Plant Communities

University of Wisconsin Arboretum, Madison

"We have dedicated the greater part of the Arboretum to a reconstruction of original Wisconsin, rather than a 'collection' of imported trees," said wildlife conservationist Aldo Leopold at a dedication ceremony for the Arboretum in 1934.

One of the most varied and popular walking places in southern Wisconsin, the Arboretum trail network embraces woodlands, prairies, and wetlands. In keeping with Leopold's vision, this place is unique. It is a collection of whole ecological communities, many of which are now in a middle stage of development.

Description and special features. Trails radiate from several parking lots within the Arboretum. Stop first at the McKay Center located on Longenecker Drive, a spur of McCaffrey Drive (also often called Arboretum Drive), for maps and additional information.

Begun in 1932 with the acquisition of a run-down 245-acre farm, the Arboretum has grown into a 1,280-acre laboratory and classroom for university students and the general public. Some highlights follow:

Curtis Prairie. The 60-acre parcel just south of the McKay Center is the world's oldest restored tallgrass prairie. Trails border and cross it so that, especially in late summer, you may experience nearly total immersion in head-high grasses and other prairie flora similar to what pioneers experienced when crossing the Great Plains. *Greene Prairie,* 45 acres in the southern part of the Grady Tract, is also a restored native prairie.

Noe Woods. Just south of the Seminole Highway entrance, this oak forest contains some examples dating back to the time of original settlement.

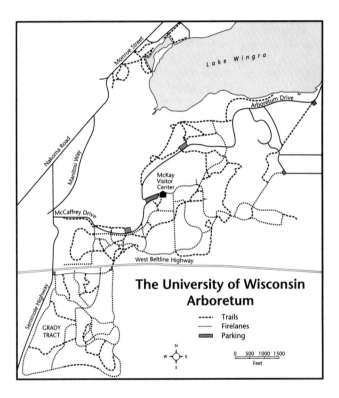

The University of Wisconsin Arboretum

----- Trails
.... Firelanes
▅ Parking

0   500 1000 1500
Feet

McKay Visitor Center

Lake Wingra

Monroe Street

Arboretum Drive

Nakoma Road

Manitou Way

McCaffrey Drive

West Beltline Highway

Seminole Highway

GRADY TRACT

Gallistel and Wingra Woods. These 77 acres of woods are slowly being converted to examples of forests of sugar maples and basswood like those commonly found in northern Wisconsin. Several Indian Effigy Mounds, constructed by Woodland Indians who lived here between 1000 B.C. and A.D. 600, are located along trails. Waterfowl often congregate in a large spring located next to the lakeside trail bordering Wingra Woods.

Longenecker Gardens. These 50 acres of ornamental plantings include lilacs and flowering crabs, a special springtime attraction. Labels identify the many tree and shrub varieties.

Degree of difficulty. Most of the 20 miles of trails are wide and well-maintained natural turf, sand, or gravel. Wood chips pave some damp areas. Trails are generally flat or gently sloping.

How to get there. The Arboretum has three major access points. (1) At the junction of Mills and Wingra Streets, several short blocks west of Park Street, on Madison's near southwest side; (2) from the Seminole Highway exit off the West Beltline, go north 0.3 mile to the entrance on the right; (3) from the Seminole Highway exit, go south over the Beltline to the four-way stop. The entrance to the Grady Tract is on the left. A pedestrian tunnel goes from the northeast corner of the Grady Tract, underneath the Beltline, to the Arboretum proper. To get to trailheads located north and east of the McKay Center, enter the Arboretum from the Mills-Wingra intersection. A gate at the McKay Center blocks the road to through traffic except from noon to 6 P.M. Sundays.

When open. Trails and landscaped areas are open to the public without charge the year around from 7 A.M. to 10 P.M. McKay Center offices and exhibit area are open from 9 A.M. to 4 P.M. weekdays and 12:30 to 4 P.M. weekends. The center is closed holidays.

To protect plants and animals, Arboretum management prohibits pets, wheeled vehicles on trails (except wheelchairs), picnicking, swimming, hunting, fishing, fires, sports, and radios. Visitors are asked to stay on trails and firelanes and not to remove natural materials.

Facilities. Parking. Flush toilets are located in the McKay Center.

Other points of interest in area

Vilas Park and Zoo has a swimming beach on Lake Wingra, picnic shelters, ice skating on the ponds, and a lot of open, grassy area, as well as some very nice shaded, paved walking paths along the park's north side. The zoo is medium size, has a good variety of animals, and is well maintained. It also includes a children's petting zoo.

Wingra Park adjoins the Arboretum on the west shore of Lake Wingra. Canoes are available for rent there.

6 Urban Park Trail Leads to Indian Mounds and Scenic Overlook

Governor Nelson State Park, Lake Mendota lakeshore northeast of Middleton

Named for Gaylord Nelson, governor, senator, and a leading environmentalist, this newest state park borders 10,000-acre Lake Mendota. On the 3.5 miles of trail you'll see several kinds of Indian mounds and view Madison's largest lake from a strategically placed overlook.

In addition to hiking and crosscountry skiing, the day-use park offers all the recreational opportunities of the lake: swimming and sunbathing at the 500-foot-long sand beach, fishing, sailing, and sailboarding, as well as power boating.

Description and special features. Three trails wind through the park:

The *Wakanda Trail* is best for hiking. It loops through a hardwood forest of old white and black oaks. From this 1.65-mile trail you'll see a 358-foot "panther" Indian effigy mound, believed to have been built by the Woodland Mound Builders between A.D. 500 and 1200. There are also about half a dozen conical mounds near the southernmost portion of the trail.

On a scenic overlook on this trail, an information station explains how the four large lakes in the Madison area were formed from glacial Lake Yahara, which was 12 feet higher and covered all the area the four lakes now occupy, plus much more.

The *Indianola Trail* actually is an additional long loop of the Wakanda trail. Its 2.35 miles wind through the original abandoned farm the park occupies, including several acres of restored prairie.

The *Olbrich Trail* provides a 0.2-mile shortcut to the parking lot for those who do not wish to retract their steps.

Degree of difficulty. Trails are wide but unsurfaced. The Wakanda trail is steeply sloped in places and can be slippery when wet.

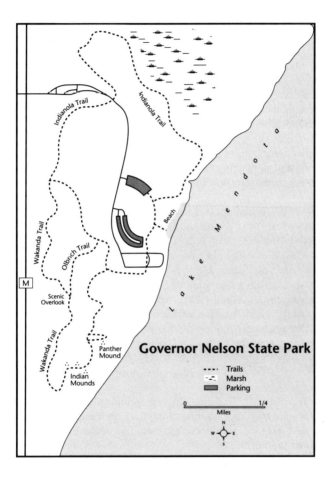

Governor Nelson State Park

- - - - Trails
~~~~ Marsh
▓▓▓ Parking

0   1/4
Miles

Lake Mendota

Indianola Trail

Wakanda Trail

Olbrich Trail

Scenic Overlook

Panther Mound

Indian Mounds

Beach

M

How to get there. From Middleton go northeast on County M for about 2.5 miles; or, from the intersection of County M and State Highway 113 go west for about 3 miles. The park entrance is to the east.

When open. The year around from 6 A.M. to 11 P.M.

Facilities. Parking, picnic shelters, flush toilets, swimming beach, bathhouses with solar-heated showers, and four-stall boat launch. The park offers an excellent fish cleaning facility near the boat launch with large metal table and electric waste disposer. No camping is allowed in this day-use park.

Other points of interest in area

Mendota County Park, also on the lake about 2 miles southwest on County M, offers camping. Sites are granted on a first-come first-served basis.

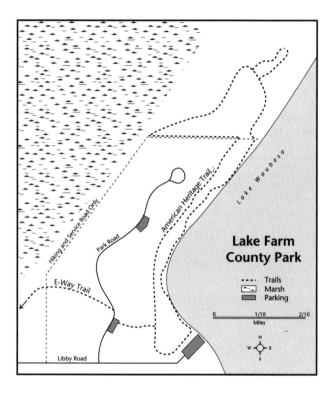

Lake Farm
County Park

- - - - Trails
Marsh
Parking

Lake Waubesa

American Heritage Trail

Park Road

Hiking and Service Road Only

E-Way Trail

Libby Road

0   1/10   2/10
Miles

N
W   E
S

7 Prehistoric Native Americans Congregated Here

American Heritage Trail, Lake Farm County Park

The spirits of civilizations past may be with you as you walk among important archaeological digs in this lakeside park.

Description and special features. The American Heritage Trail starts with a spur at the parking lot that goes to the main trail. The trail follows the shore of Lake Waubesa for about one-half mile through prairie and oak woodland. It then turns left and loops back to the spur. You can also enter the trail from the boat ramp parking lot.

Other trails in the park go mostly through restored native prairie. These are especially worthwhile to take from midsummer to late fall, when many flowering plants reach maturity. The trails are part of the Nine Springs E-Way Corridor, a natural resource area along the southern border of Madison.

The location of Lake Farm Park, on the shore of Lake Waubesa and bordering marshes, made it especially attractive to Native Americans throughout prehistory. Archaeologists have identified and saved for future study some 32 sites where prehistoric Indians lived. They've found evidence that the location was used as early as 5000 B.C., and perhaps earlier, by Late Paleo-Indian cultures. Indians of the Late Archaic stage (3000 to 500 B.C.) probably were the first to settle here, artifacts unearthed seem to indicate. The area was inhabited on and off by various Indian groups into the Late Woodland stage to about A.D. 1000.

To protect them from looters, archaeological sites are not specifically identified. However, you can see mounds along the trail indicating digging locations.

A number of informational stations on the trail tell about the life of early inhabitants and the reasons they settled in the area.

Degree of difficulty. Mostly flat, wide and easy, the trails are well maintained except for a few spots with minor ruts. Grass covers most trails, with wood chips in lower areas. The American Heritage Trail is about 1.7 miles long. Other trails in the park are an additional 2 miles.

How to get there. From the South Towne Drive exit off Madison's Beltline (U.S. 12–18), go south on Raywood Road for 0.8 mile, then east (left) on Moorland Road, which becomes Lake Farm Road, for about 1 mile, then left on Libby Road for 0.6 mile to the park on the left.

When open. Dane County parks are open daily the year around from 5 A.M. to 10 P.M.

Facilities. The county recently fully developed the 295-acre Lake Farm Park. Facilities include a paved boat ramp with docks and fish-cleaning building, flush toilets, picnic shelters and tables, children's playgrounds, horseshoe pits, and volleyball net. County builders transformed an observation tower from an old silo. There is no fee, and camping is not allowed in the park.

Other points of interest in area

Goodland County Park, a favorite for picnicking because of its shade trees and beautiful lake view, is also located on the west shore of Lake Waubesa, about 1.5 miles south (or 3 miles by road) of Lake Farm Park. It has a swimming beach, tennis courts, basketball hoops, softball diamond, and boat launch. Take Lake Farm Road south from Libby Road to Goodland Park Road. Go east to the park entrance.

8 Trail Leads to Indian Mounds among Towering White Oaks

White Oak Nature Trail, Lake Kegonsa State Park

Pioneers called Lake Kegonsa "First Lake" because it was the first of four major lakes they encountered in the Madison area when traveling northwest. Later, they adopted the Winnebago name *Kegonsa,* which means "lake of many fishes."

Established in 1962, the 342-acre park on the lake's northeast shore offers a variety of hiking trails through woods and restored prairie. The White Oak Nature Trail winds among oak trees estimated to be 200 years old. They stand like pillars on all sides, providing an exhilarating hiking experience.

Description and special features. About 1.3 miles long, this trail loops through a forest that is unusual in that it consists of mostly a single species of oak. A portion of the trail also borders a plantation of white pines.

It passes near linear Indian mounds, constructed by Woodland Culture Indians between 800 and 1,200 years ago, at two locations. It's surprising to find the mounds this far from the lake, which borders the other side of the park. Usually such mounds are located a lot closer to open water.

Occasional informational stops identify trees and shrubs, though some signs were damaged or missing during my autumn walk.

Degree of difficulty. The trail has a natural surface and is wide, with only gentle slopes. It may be slippery when wet.

How to get there. From I-90 take exit number 147, 4 miles north of Stoughton, go south on County N for 0.6 miles, then west on Koshkonong Road for 1.7 miles, then south on Door Creek Road for 0.9 mile to the park entrance on the right.

When open. The year around. A state park sticker is required, though enforcement is sporadic except during the summer.

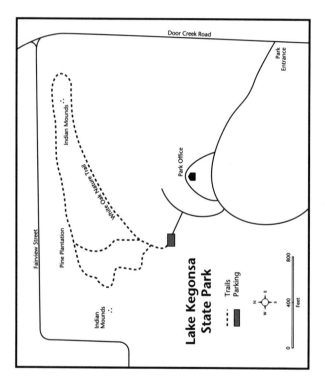

Lake Kegonsa State Park

Door Creek Road

Park Entrance

Indian Mounds

White Oak Nature Trail

Park Office

Fairview Street

Pine Plantation

Indian Mounds

Trails
Parking

N
W · E
S

0   400   800
Feet

Facilities. Parking in several lots, 80 family campsites and a large group campsite, trailer dumping facility, flush toilets, drinking water, and picnic tables are available. The park includes a beach and a boat launch.

Other points of interest in area

About 4 miles south of the park, Stoughton is one of the largest communities of Norwegian settlers in Wisconsin. In mid-May the Syttende Mai celebration features a parade and exhibits of Norwegian crafts. For details call the chamber of commerce at 608-873-7912.

9 Take This Trail to an Unexpected Discovery

Yahara Heights–Cherokee Marsh, Madison

As any veteran walker knows, once in a while you'll hike down a trail you haven't explored and be delightfully surprised by what you discover. Finding the trail into the Yahara River–Cherokee Marsh area that's on Dane County's park brochure completely grown over one summer day, I looked for another access trail. The one I found at the end of Riverview Drive led to an unmarked Indian effigy mound where the trail reached the riverbank.

Park authorities no doubt have the mound's location well charted, but I still enjoyed the thrill of discovery at the end of this little-used trail.

Description and special features. The two-lane trail crosses rolling, partially wooded terrain for about 400 yards from its beginning to the river. It then bends left and follows the river-bank generally northeast to a rather indeterminate end. The effigy mound of a long-tailed creature is on the left just past the bend.

Degree of difficulty. The trail, probably a former maintenance road, is unpaved but fairly wide with only gentle slopes. It narrows and becomes grown over in places along the river.

How to get there. From State Highway 113 north of Madison, just north of its junction with County M, take River Road to the east for about 0.6 mile to Riverview Drive on the right, then about 0.2 mile to the trailhead at the end of Riverview.

The trail I found to be grown over, but which may be maintained better in the future, enters the 145-acre county-owned site from a parking lot just east of the intersection of Highway 113 and County M.

When open. The year around. Probably impassable at times during the winter.

Facilities. None. Park along the road at the trailhead.

Other points of interest in area

Follow Highway 113 into Madison's north side to Lakeview Woods, a heavily wooded 27-acre conservancy just behind the Lakeview Annex Building at 1202–1206 Northport Drive. A hiking trail through the woods provides a stark contrast to surrounding residential areas. You'll get a great view of Lake Mendota from this highest point on the north side of the city. A 1991 windstorm damaged many of the old oaks and other hardwoods. The county parks department was to schedule cleanup as funds became available, a department representative said.

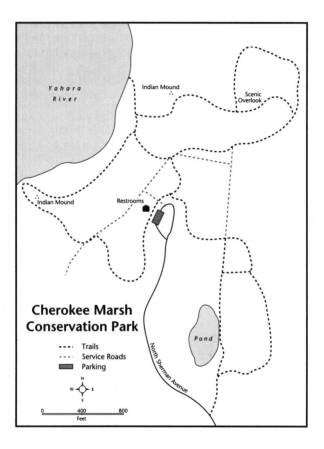

Y a h a r a
R i v e r

Indian Mound

Scenic
Overlook

Indian Mound

Restrooms

**Cherokee Marsh
Conservation Park**

- - - Trails
- - - Service Roads
Parking

N
W   E
S

0   400   800
Feet

P o n d

North Sherman Avenue

10 Trails Lace Natural Area That City Preserves from Development

Cherokee Marsh Conservation Park, Sherman Avenue Unit, Madison

The city purchased this natural area, which was threatened by development, in the 1960s. In an environmental education work-learn project, high school students have assisted the Parks Division in developing trails, including a long boardwalk through a section of the marsh bordering the Yahara River.

Description and special features. Nearly three miles of trails lace the Sherman Avenue portion of the park. One loop of the trail climbs a low hill of sandstone bedrock covered by glacial till with many glacial erratics strewn about. The trail passes a well-preserved conical Indian mound and leads to an overlook atop the hill.

In another loop, take a 1,500-foot boardwalk through peat marshes that border the Yahara River. In early postglacial times, Cherokee Marsh was a lake. Peat settled into the lake and is now as much as 30 feet deep in places, says Cy Wydstrand of the city's Parks Division. The boardwalk leads to the tip of a peninsula with another conical mound that is an Indian burial site, according to a marker there.

Degree of difficulty. Portions of the trails on grasslands and prairie are wide and mowed. Trail builders have paved forested portions with gravel and wood chips. Through the marsh, the boardwalk provides easy going. You'll hike over gentle slopes on the hill. Hiking trails are not groomed in winter.

How to get there. In northeast Madison, take Sherman Avenue north of Wheeler Road over a gravel road to a parking lot at its terminus.

When open. During daylight hours the year around. Park authorities close an iron gate near the park entrance at dusk.

Facilities. Parking. Flush toilets, in a building adjacent the parking lot, are open the year around.

Other points of interest in area

A separate portion of the park, called the southern unit by the Parks Division, has trails for both hiking and cross country skiing. A road that is open from spring to about November 15 leads to a parking lot and a ramp for small boats. You may enter at the intersection of Wheeler and School roads, where there is parking for a few cars, or at a spur farther east on Wheeler Road, where you may park along the road.

11 Take a Quiet Route over a Glacial Moraine

Brooklyn Wildlife Area, southern Dane County

👟 👟 👟

If you enjoy a walk through hill and prairie in solitude, you'll usually get it in this little-known but pleasant walking place. Part of it has been designated a segment of the Ice Age National Scenic Trail.

Description and special features. From a roadside parking lot the trail offers several routes over a glacier-formed moraine, oak forested in this location, that runs southeast to northwest through Dane County. The opposite side of the moraine reveals a grassy prairie, much of which was reclaimed from the plow, that borders Story Creek. The area is a Pittman-Robertson wildlife restoration project of the Department of Natural Resources.

Degree of difficulty. The trails are natural turf but wide and easy to follow with moderate slopes.

How to get there. From Madison, go south on Fish Hatchery Road (County D) for about 8 miles beyond County M, and then go 0.8 mile on County DD. A parking lot on the left is poorly marked and easy to miss. If you reach the Green County line, you've gone too far.

When open. The year around. The trail may be impassable in winter. The area is open to hunters during spring and fall hunting seasons. Wear bright clothing then to avoid becoming an accidental target.

Facilities. Parking.

Other points of interest in area

About one-half mile south of D's intersection with M, on the right, a natural history marker tells about the glacier-formed "Swan Pond" 100 yards from the road, where whistling swans stop during their migrations.

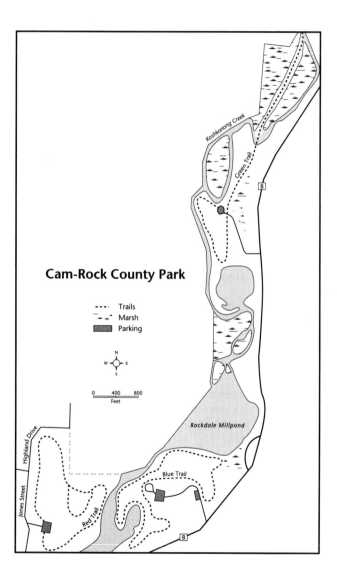

Cam-Rock County Park

- - - - Trails
△◣ ◥▷ Marsh
▨ Parking

N
W ⊕ E
S

0   400   800
Feet

Koshkonong Creek

Green Trail

B

Rockdale Millpond

Highland Drive

Jones Street

Red Trail

Blue Trail

B

12 Three Creekside Trails Are near Two Picturesque Villages

Cam-Rock County Park, Cambridge and Rockdale

A 300-acre park borders gently flowing Koshkonong Creek and lies between two picturesque villages: busy Cambridge with its pottery factories and craft shops and sleepy Rockdale, a historic place built around an old grist mill.

Description and special features. Each of three trails in the three-part park loops around a centrally located parking lot.

The *Green Trail,* in the northernmost section of the park, follows an old railroad bed through forest and marsh and loops around a ball field and picnic grounds along the creek. Notice the abundant hickory trees—some very old—on this trail. The age of the abandoned railroad bed is indicated by oaks—some probably up to 75 years old—growing on the right of way.

The *Blue Trail* borders the millpond formed by a dam in the creek and goes out onto a peninsula, providing greeting-card-like views of the village of Rockdale.

On the *Red Trail,* you'll descend from the parking lot to the pond and then crisscross up a wooded hill, from which you'll be treated to panoramic views of the pond on the left and the village on the right.

Degree of difficulty. The Green Trail is mostly flat and has the firm foundation of the railroad bed covered with crushed limestone. A couple of moderate hills on the Blue Trail provide more strenuous exercise. Though recently covered with wood chips, the trail at the tip of the peninsula may be soggy during wet weather. The slope of the Red Trail will test your endurance, though the climb is worth the view. All trails are wide and, except for the railroad bed, unpaved.

How to get there. From U.S. 12 in Cambridge, go south on County B for about a mile, along the east side of Koshkonong Creek. The entrance leading to the Green Trail is on the right.

A second entrance and parking lot, accessing the Blue Trail, is several miles farther south, also on the right. To find the Red Trail, take Jones Street north out of Rockdale west of the mill-pond. The entrance to the parking lot is on the right just north of the village.

When open. Dane County parks are open from 5 A.M. to 10 P.M. the year around. Cross-country skiers ply the trails when there is snow cover, and hiking on groomed trails is discouraged. Parking lots are open from about the first weekend in May to the last weekend in October and during skiing weather. Hikers may park outside the gates and walk in when parking lots are closed.

Facilities. Each of the three sections of the park has its own picnic shelter and flush toilets. There are also canoe launches, playgrounds, and a softball field.

Other points of interest in area

In Cambridge, the Rowe Pottery Works produces salt-glaze pottery and accessories. Its factory outlet store at 217 Main Street and the Rockdale Union Stoneware Retail Store at 137 Main Street are worthwhile stops.

Hoard Historical Museum and Dairy Shrine, 407 Merchants Avenue in Fort Atkinson, is named for former governor and dairy farming pioneer W. D. Hoard. Exhibits tell about the history of dairy farming in Wisconsin, the Blackhawk War of 1832, and Native American life before the advent of Europeans. A fee is charged.

The Fireside Restaurant and Playhouse, also in Fort Atkinson on State Highway 26, is widely known for its live productions in a theater-in-the-round. It's open the year around Wednesday through Sunday. For information about current performances call 414-536-9505.

13 Walk Where Indians Lived and Pioneers Prayed

Indian Lake County Park

🥾 🥾

   The trails in this park offer discovery of several kinds. Climb to a small stone chapel built by a pioneer homesteader after a diptheria epidemic. Or find chips of stone remaining from Native American toolmaking.

   Recently developed, Indian Lake County Park offers a network of trails through hilly forests and prairie. It provides excellent hiking and a challenge for cross-country skiers.

Description and special features. Trails in the 422-acre park wind through mostly hardwood forest with oaks, aspen, hickory, and birch on north slopes. A new trail, a segment of the Ice Age National Scenic Trail, goes around the lake. It includes 900 feet of elevated boardwalk over the shallow end of the lake.

   A finger of the last continental glacier oozed from the main ice mass into the valley to form Indian Lake. As you hike through the hills you will see rock outcroppings typical of Wisconsin's Driftless Area, which was not covered by the glacier. However, the valley contains glacial deposits of drift (rocks and till), and a thin layer of till also covers surrounding hilltops.

   An Indian village once occupied the shore of the lake. Follow the main trail east from the parking lot and you may find chips of chert along the edge of the path, likely remaining from Indian toolmaking.

   The highlight of the trail system is a small chapel, St. Mary of the Oaks, built in 1857 by pioneer farmer John Endres. It's located on the top of a bluff accessible by trail and, for the steeper portions, stairs. In the winter of 1856–57, Endres's entire family contracted diphtheria during one of the worst epidemics to hit the state, historians report. When the illness seemed at its most severe, Endres climbed the hill behind his farm and prayed. He vowed that, if his family were spared, he would build a chapel on the spot overlooking the lake. His family recovered.

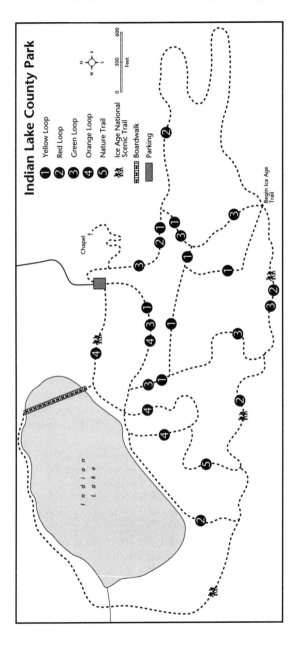

Indian Lake County Park

1 Yellow Loop
2 Red Loop
3 Green Loop
4 Orange Loop
5 Nature Trail

Ice Age National Scenic Trail

Boardwalk

Parking

Chapel

Indian Lake

Begin Ice Age Trail

The following spring Endres and his son, Peter, began to build the shrine, hauling stone to the top of the hill. He carved the altar that remains in the chapel today. Several generations later in 1923 the land was sold, but subsequent owners maintained the shrine and even wrote into the deed that it must be "kept up . . . by heirs and assigns forever." Eventually, Dane County purchased the land for use as a park.

Degree of difficulty. Trails in the park total 9 miles. The longest is 4.5 miles and the shortest 1.3 miles. While trails vary in difficulty, the terrain is generally hilly. I found the most strenuous climb to be to the top of the bluff where Endres's chapel is located, though other trails also are steep. Trails are wide and usually in excellent condition, with mostly grassy turf.

How to get there. From U.S. 12 about 20 miles north of Middleton, go west on State Highway 19 for 2.1 miles to the entrance of the park on the left. To launch a small boat (only electric motors allowed), follow Highway 19 another 0.9 mile.

When open. 5 A.M. to 10 P.M. daily the year around.

Facilities. A small picnic shelter and water well with hand pump are located on the side of the hill. Pit toilets are near the parking lot.

Other points of interest in area

Old Halfway Prairie School, the oldest existing school building in Dane County, sits among shade trees on the north side of State Highway 19 about six miles to the west of Indian Lake Park. Operated from 1844 to 1961, it received its name because it was halfway between Mineral Point and Portage on a route traveled by early miners. Visitors may view the authentically restored interior from Memorial Day to Labor Day from 1 P.M. to 5 P.M. Sundays and holidays.

Festge County Park is located near U.S. 14 about 1.5 miles west of Cross Plains. It has a nature trail, a 100-foot-high overlook, and a marker telling about Wisconsin's Driftless Area. Salmo Pond, across Highway 14 from the park, has a barrier-free fishing pier and a swimming area.

14 Trail through Donated Park Provides River Valley Views

Phil's Woods County Park, northwestern Dane County

The La Follettes provided Wisconsin a legacy not only of progressive political institutions but also a fine park that has a hiking and cross-country ski trail with a spectacular view of the Wisconsin River valley. The 37-acre Phil's Woods was part of Philip F. La Follette's farm. His family contributed it to the state, which in turn transferred it to Dane County's jurisdiction for a natural resource area.

Description and special features. About two-thirds mile long, the trail begins at Dunlap Hollow Road and loops up one side of a hill and down the other, bending around to close the loop. Most of the trail is through hardwood forest, including a mature stand of birch and many white oaks.

From a small prairie at the top of the hill, the view to the north takes in Sauk City, Prairie du Sac, the large hydroelectric dam on the river, and across the river the Badger Ordnance "powder plant" and the Baraboo Hills.

Degree of difficulty. The trail is unpaved and steep, but wide. Slopes may be difficult to negotiate in wet weather.

How to get there. From Sauk City go south about 2 miles on U.S. 12 to Dunlap Hollow Road. Go right 1.2 miles to the park on the right. Park on the side of the road. There is a large sign at the trailhead, but it's easy to miss while driving up a hill.

When open. The year around.

Facilities. Phil's Woods has no facilities. The charm is in its quiet, undeveloped seclusion.

Other points of interest in area

You may rent a canoe in nearby Sauk City to see more of the Wisconsin River. Bender's Bluffview Canoe Rentals, 614 Spruce Street, or Sauk Prarie Canoe Rentals, 932 Water Street, will rent you a canoe and pick you up downriver at the end of your trip.

For a wintertime activity, view the bald eagles that feed in open water of the Wisconsin River bordering Sauk City and Prairie du Sac. One of the best viewing locations is just below the Prairie du Sac dam, just off State Highway 78 about a mile north of Prairie du Sac. During the winter, these eagles are in the south of their range, which stretches to the Arctic Circle.

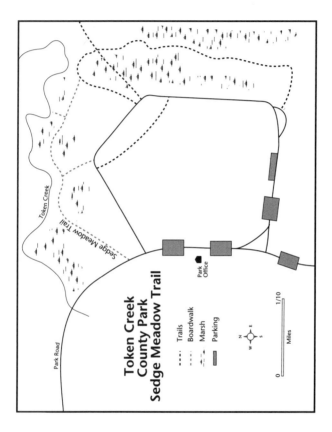

Token Creek
County Park
Sedge Meadow Trail

Token Creek

Sedge Meadow Trail

Park Road

Park Office

Trails
Boardwalk
Marsh
Parking

N
W — E
S

0 _____ 1/10
Miles

15 On a Boardwalk Get a Unique View of a Sedge Meadow

Sedge Meadow Trail, Token Creek County Park

👟 👟 👟

Description and special features. The trail follows Token Creek, a tributary of the Yahara River, through a lush sedge meadow and prairie basin growing on rich alkaline peat deposits laid down when the continental glacier was melting. Boardwalk construction of a portion of the trail enables the walker to get an unusually good view of sedge meadow and prairie flora.

Look for pussy willows in the spring, lavender asters and stemmed cup plants in the summer, and jewelweed seed pods that explode when touched in the fall. Spring also finds the woodcock doing its spectacular "sky dance" to attract a mate.

Degree of difficulty. The first quarter mile of the trail is a boardwalk that, while uneven because of settling supports, still provides safe, comfortable walking. The boardwalk connects to broad natural-turf trails that loop throughout the 295-acre park. Starting in 1993, portions of the boardwalk will at times be closed for reconstruction, says Ken LePine, county parks system director.

Trails through the peat bogs will be soft and possibly muddy during wet weather, but others on higher terrain are grassy and firm. Some of these trails are also bridle paths, so step carefully or pay the consequences.

How to get there. The park entrance is on the right about one-quarter mile north of the intersection of U.S. 51 and I-90–94, northeast of Madison.

When open. 5 A.M. to 10 P.M. the year around.

Facilities. Park designers have provided campsites with or without electrical hookups, plenty of picnic shelters, toilets, and running water, as well as a trailer dumping station that's open during the summer camping season. You may cross-country ski on some trails during winter.

Other points of interest in area

Go about six miles west on State Highway 19 to Schumacher Farm, just east of Waunakee on the north side of the highway. Donated to the public for development as a prairie and open-air museum, the reserve has a walking trail through a ten-acre restored native tall-grass prairie. Over 100 native species of plants are being nurtured within the prairie.

16 Riverway Project Acquires Hiker's Paradise

Blackhawk Ridge, northern Dane County

Walkers and hikers benefited in a big way when Wisconsin's Department of Natural Resources acquired this choice 523-acre property in 1991. A former commercially operated wilderness campground, the trail-laced ridge is being incorporated into the Lower Wisconsin State Riverway to protect it from development for future generations.

Description and special features. The blacktop trail to the top was the road to the former campground. It is now closed to vehicular traffic and, instead, provides an easy, though steep, way for the walker to get to the top of the ridge. Most of the other trails, totaling over ten miles, branch out from the top.

With a maximum elevation of 220 feet above the entering roadway, the ridge-top trails offer a commanding view of the Wisconsin River valley. Although the DNR's specific plans for this property were still being formulated at this writing, the master plan for the State Riverway calls for maintaining the wild character of riverside land, according to Dave Gjestson, Lower Wisconsin State Riverway coordinator. While the trails will be maintained and even extended, one of the chief features of Blackhawk will be its pristine, undisturbed character.

Limited hunting is now allowed on the property. Planners are considering including equestrian trails, since the area was a favorite of riders before state acquisition.

Degree of difficulty. The approach from the highway to the ridge is well-maintained blacktop. It took me about 15 minutes to make the half-mile climb. Other trails are wide and mostly unpaved. Some traverse steep hillsides.

How to get there. From the junction of U.S. 12 and State Highway 78 just south of Sauk City, go south on Highway 78 for two miles. At this writing the entrance was not well marked. There is space near the entrance to park a few cars.

When open. The year around. The DNR plans to groom hiking trails in winter once it obtains the necessary equipment.

Facilities. None at this writing.

Other points of interest in area

See chapter 2.14 on Phil's Woods, also in this area.

Guided tours take you through the vineyards and wine cellar of the Wollersheim Winery, established by Count Augustin Haraszthy, who is considered the father of viticulture in California. From the Wisconsin River Bridge in Sauk City, go south on U.S. 12 one-half mile to State Highway 188 and turn left. The winery is a few miles down the road, on the right.

Grant County

Afoot and light-hearted I take to the open road,
Healthy, free, the world before me,
The long brown path before me leading wherever I choose.

Walt Whitman, LEAVES OF GRASS

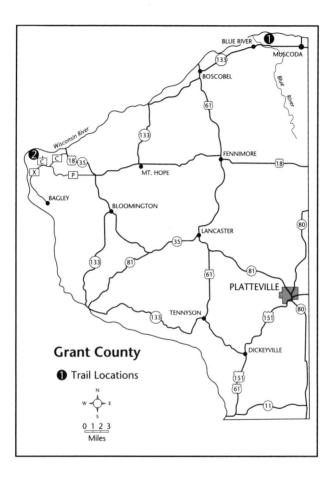

BLUE RIVER

MUSCODA

Blue River

133

BOSCOBEL

61

Wisconsin River

133

FENNIMORE

18

C
18 35

X

P

MT. HOPE

BAGLEY

BLOOMINGTON

LANCASTER

80

35

133

81

61

81

PLATTEVILLE

80

TENNYSON

133

151

DICKEYVILLE

Grant County

❶ Trail Locations

151
61

11

N
W E
S

0 1 2 3
Miles

1 Rare Plants and Animals Are Protected among Sand Dunes

Blue River Sand Barrens State Natural Area, Blue River

Tucked away from highway traffic and public notice, this quiet protected area contains—yes, in Wisconsin—prickly pear cactus plants in abundance. A globally rare flower, the prairie fame flower, also grows on these sand barrens and dunes. Another species, the poppy mallow, is protected.

Description and special features. Once an unpaved road, this trail is now legally closed to vehicular traffic, although I saw the fresh tire tracks of several apparent scofflaws during my walk there. The trail follows the border of a unique sand terrace along the edge of Wisconsin River backwaters. It is believed the terrace was part of the riverbed when the river was much higher in early postglacial times.

The barrens and blows are interspersed with more permanent dunes upon which scattered black oaks have established themselves and somehow survive. Because the sand, believed to be over 100 feet deep, does not easily hold moisture from rain or snow, plants normally associated with much drier climates thrive here. Thus the cactus and many of the grasses and lichens found in this 130-acre preserve are strangers to Wisconsin.

Degree of difficulty. The soft sand trail follows fairly level terrain, making for easy walking.

How to get there. About two miles east of Blue River or four miles west of Muscoda on State Highway 133, take Wightman Road north about one-quarter mile to the entrance of the protected area. Park along the road.

When open. The year around.

Facilities. None.

Other points of interest in area

Muscoda calls itself the Morel Capital of the World. Early every spring it hosts a festival honoring this delicate mushroom taste treat. For details contact the Chamber of Commerce at 633 North Wisconsin Avenue, Muscoda, WI 53573 (telephone 608-739-3639).

2 Park Occupies a Busy Corner in State History

Wyalusing State Park, Prairie du Chien

At the confluence of the Wisconsin and Mississippi rivers, the location of Wyalusing has made it a "busy corner" in human history for some 9,000 years. Paleo Indians probably selected the location for settlement because the rivers were means of sustenance and arteries for transportation. Indians of the Woodland and possibly Hopewell cultures built processions of effigy mounds high on the bluffs overlooking the rivers. More recent Indians considered the area neutral ground, where at least fourteen tribes settled or visited to trade.

In 1673 Father Jacques Marquette and explorer Louis Joliet, the first whites on record to discover the corner, paddled into the Mississippi "with a joy I cannot express," Marquette wrote in his journal. They were soon followed by French, and then British, trappers and fur traders, and inevitably soldiers. Miners and farmers came with their dreams of prosperity, and in 1848 the area became part of the newly formed State of Wisconsin.

One of four places in the state originally recommended for purchase as a park, Wyalusing (then called Nelson Dewey) State Park was established in 1917 and since has grown to over 2,600 acres.

Its riverside location, high bluffs, scenic views, and diverse geology and wildlife make it one of the best hiking parks in the state.

Description and special features. Wyalusing's ten hiking trails range in length from 0.5 to 3.6 miles. While I have walked the majority of trails, I found trail descriptions in the *Park Visitor* and other DNR publications to be accurate and useful as sources for much of the following descriptions.

Sugar Maple Nature Trail. A self-guided trail goes through heavy woods and into deep valleys. A short side trail leads to Rock Cave, which has a waterfall tumbling over its entrance. The trail is a 1.5-mile loop with some slopes, steps, and steep areas.

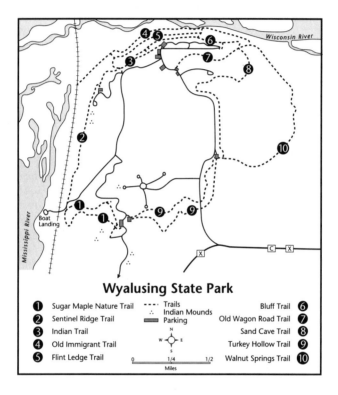

Wyalusing State Park

①	Sugar Maple Nature Trail	Bluff Trail	⑥
②	Sentinel Ridge Trail	Old Wagon Road Trail	⑦
③	Indian Trail	Sand Cave Trail	⑧
④	Old Immigrant Trail	Turkey Hollow Trail	⑨
⑤	Flint Ledge Trail	Walnut Springs Trail	⑩

- - - Trails
∴ Indian Mounds
▭ Parking

N
W—◇—E
S

0   1/4   1/2
Miles

Sentinel Ridge Trail. 👟 👟 👟 This trail offers spectacular views along the length of the riverside bluffs. About midway is a monument to the extinct passenger pigeon. In the same area the trail follows a train of effigy, linear, conical, and combined Indian mounds. Informational signs describe how Indians used native plants and animals. The 1.6-mile trail is level and easy on the ridge but becomes steep and rocky as it descends toward a boat landing.

Indian Trail. 👟 👟 👟 👟 This trail was actually used by Native Americans before whites arrived. Mostly through woods, it descends from the top of the bluff to the river, connecting to several other trails along the way. You'll encounter steep slopes and steps along its 0.5-mile length.

Old Immigrant Trail. 👟 👟 In the past this trail led to a ferry across the Mississippi and it was used by settlers going westward. Its easy, mostly level route goes 1.5 miles along the bank of the Wisconsin and its backwaters.

Flint Ledge Trail. 👟 👟 👟 👟 Meandering along the face of the lower bluff, this trail has many crevices and small caves to see on the way. You'll see veins of flint, or chert, in the rock wall. Indians prized them as sources of material for arrowheads and tools. The 0.8-mile trail is narrow and goes near drop-offs.

Bluff Trail. 👟 👟 👟 Going high along the Wisconsin River bluffs for 0.9 mile, this trail offers some great views. Steep stairs lead from the trail up to Treasure Cave.

Old Wagon Road Trail. 👟 👟 Animal-drawn wagons followed this gently sloped old road 0.8 mile through heavy woods down the bluff to Walnut Eddy, a settlement that now, of course, is abandoned.

Sand Cave Trail. 👟 👟 👟 You'll walk through heavy woods to Sand Cave and over several streams along this 1.7-mile route. A small waterfall is a highlight. Expect to encounter some steps, steepness, and drop-offs.

Turkey Hollow Trail. 👟 Look for wild turkeys and other wildlife in the open prairie and in pine and oak woods along this 3.2-mile loop. You can relax along this wide, grassy, sometimes gently sloping path.

Walnut Springs Trail. 👟 👟 A gently rolling, mostly grassy path, it winds for 2.6 miles through maple woods and along the side of a deep ravine on an old logging road. Crossing a stream several times, going along the river bottom with its huge walnut trees, and bordering a white pine plantation, this is one of the most varied and interesting of Wyalusing's trails.

Degree of difficulty. See individual descriptions.

How to get there. From Prairie du Chien go south 6 miles on U.S. 18, then west 6 miles on County C.

When open. The year around from 6 A.M. to 11 P.M., except for overnight campers. Park staff encourages wintertime use.

Facilities. Besides hiking, camping is one of the featured activities of this park. You may wish to use one of two family campgrounds with a total of 132 sites, of which 32 have electricity. Two sites are dedicated for use by handicapped campers. Showers and a recreational vehicle dumping station are provided. There are also group camping sites.

You can launch your boat from a wide, blacktop ramp. Other facilities include a nature center, year-round toilets, and year-round water sources. The park also has tennis courts, a softball field, and a bluff-top picnic shelter.

Other points of interest in area

Villa Louis, a Victorian mansion in Prairie du Chien, was built in 1870 by the widow and son of Hercules Dousman, one of the area's first settlers. Authentic period furnishings and decor bring back an opulent Victorian lifestyle. Open from 9 A.M. to 5 P.M. May 1–October 31. A fee is charged.

Stonefield Village, about 30 miles south of the park near Cassville, was reconstructed by the State Historical Society to depict life in a Wisconsin village in the 1890s. Buildings include a bank, newspaper office, blacksmith shop, and livery stable.

The village is part of Nelson Dewey State Park, named for Wisconsin's first governor and located on the grounds of a mansion he built. The park has camping, Indian mounds, several miles of hiking trails, and a self-guided nature trail. A separate fee is charged for Stonefield Village, which is open from late May to early October. The park, located two miles west of Cassville on County VV, is open the year around.

Many who see Indian mounds in Wisconsin have questions about these archaeological treasures. Effigy Mounds National Monument, nearby in Iowa, preserves many kinds of Indian mounds within its 1,475 acres. A visitor center contains a small museum that explains the mounds and shows artifacts taken from some of them. A 14-minute film tells about the Native Americans of the Woodland culture who built them. The monument includes 11 miles of hiking trails, is open the year around, and charges a small fee. Cross the Mississippi River on the U.S. 18 bridge at Prairie du Chien to Marquette, Iowa, then go north 3 miles on State Highway 76.

Green County

I wish I could walk for a day and a night,
And find me at dawn in a desolate place
With never the rut of a road in sight,
Nor the roof of a house, nor the eyes of a face.

Edna St. Vincent Millay, DEPARTURE

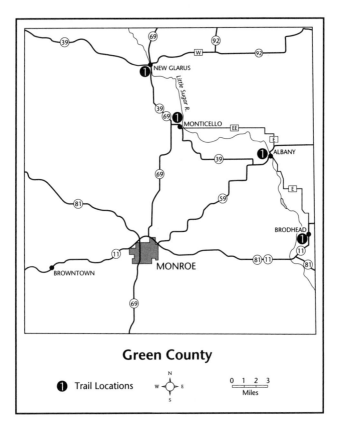

Green County

1 Trail Locations

N
W ✦ E
S

0 1 2 3
Miles

1 Walk Where Wood-fired Steam Trains Once Chugged

Sugar River State Trail

When Albany, Wisconsin, pioneer James Campbell first organized the Sugar River Valley Railroad in 1855, he had no idea his efforts would result in the construction of a scenic biking and hiking trail through the valley of the gently flowing river 119 years later.

As you follow the Sugar River State Trail from village to village through the serene pastures of Green County, you will walk where wood-fired steam trains once transported people and goods over this lifeline of commerce up and down the valley. Use of the railroad declined and eventually ceased in 1972. A national leader in establishing trails on old railroad beds, Wisconsin's Department of Natural Resources approved the purchase of the 23-mile, 100-foot-wide strip of land the same year. Formally dedicated in 1974, the trail was used by 40,000 people the first year.

Description and special features. Part of the Ice Age National Scenic Trail and also a National Recreation Trail, the first section begins at the old depot in the Swiss village of New Glarus and follows the Little Sugar River through the New Glarus Public Hunting Grounds to a point 1.5 miles north of Monticello. In spring you'll see the white blossoms of wild plums and elderberries, and the greenish-white flowers of bur cucumber. The presence of willow and aspen trees reflects a recent disturbing of the soil when the trail was built.

Before reaching the village of Monticello, the trail runs along the base of a bluff that is at the edge of the Driftless Area. The area just north and east of here was covered by a glacier 30,000 years ago, but not by the more recent Laurentide Ice Sheet. A rock cut exposes layers of St. Peter sandstone laid down 450 million years ago.

Beyond Monticello the trail traverses the Albany Wildlife Area. Watch for ducks, pheasants, and such songbirds as the goldfinch and cardinal. The green heron, a wading bird with a

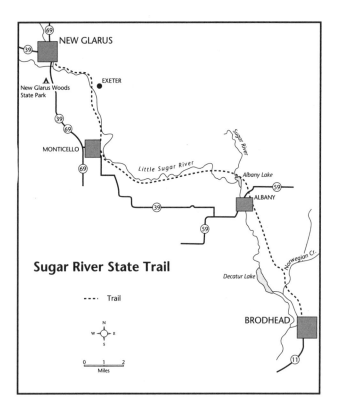

69 NEW GLARUS

39

⛺ New Glarus Woods
State Park

• EXETER

39

69

MONTICELLO

69

Little Sugar River

Sugar River

Albany Lake

59

39

ALBANY

59

Norwegian Cr.

Sugar River State Trail

- - - Trail

Decatur Lake

N
W ✦ E
S

BRODHEAD

0   1   2
Miles

11

long chestnut-colored neck, also has been sighted here, according to DNR literature.

Among 14 bridges crossing the Sugar River and its tributaries are three in this section crossing Burgy Creek, Hammerly Creek, and the Little Sugar River, which flows into the Sugar River. A fourth bridge, crossing the Sugar River, is the longest of the trail.

After passing through the village of Albany, the trail leaves the railroad grade for about one-half mile, going through hardwood and pine forests instead. The railway right-of-way here was never owned by the railroad and reverted to the owner of the adjacent farm when the railroad was abandoned. The DNR reports that the edible morel mushroom can be found near the bypass.

Some 2.5 miles north of Brodhead, you'll cross a covered bridge over Norwegian Creek. A replica of a bridge that once crossed the Sugar River south of Brodhead, this bridge was built in 1984 by volunteers from the city.

Degree of difficulty. Hard-packed limestone screenings pave a former railroad bed with less than 1 percent grade to provide a trail that's easy to walk or bike. Cross-country skiing and snowmobiling are also permitted.

How to get there. You may access the trail at any of the four towns along the way: New Glarus, Monticello, Albany, or Brodhead.

When open. From 6 A.M. to 11 P.M. daily. Hikers are not charged the nominal fee required of bicycle riders over age 17.

Facilities. Trail headquarters in the old depot at New Glarus has a concession stand and toilets, and you may park in the adjacent lot. Each of the four communities has parks and restaurants within a mile of the trail.

Other points of interest in area

Swiss Village Museum, at Seventh Avenue and Sixth Street in New Glarus, contains a miniature replica of the 1840s village complete with a church, cheese factory, and blacksmith shop. It's open from May through October. A fee is charged.

The "Old Lead Road," now County N, runs through New Glarus Woods State Park, 1.5 miles south of New Glarus on State Highway 69. It connected Milwaukee and Mineral Point and was originally a Winnebago Indian trail. The park has 18 family and 14 primitive bicycle campsites, plus a 1.2-mile hiking trail and a nature trail.

Iowa County

I have been taking daily walks for some thirty years and I conclude that, though habit-forming, the practice is not quickly fatal.

John Kieran, A Spring Walk

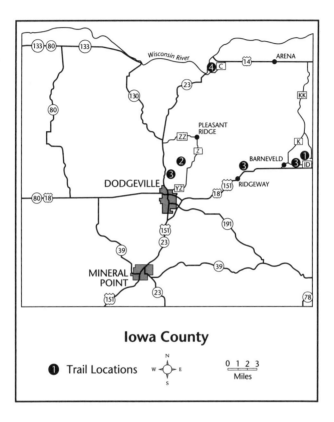

Iowa County

❶ Trail Locations

N
W—✦—E
S

0 1 2 3
Miles

1 Trails and Facilities Will Please the Whole Family

Blue Mound State Park, Blue Mounds

👟 👟 👟

If you like to take your spouse, pack up the kids, and make a day of it when you go hiking, Blue Mound Park is the place to go. It has not only a variety of trails but also two observation towers, nature center, picnic grounds, and even a swimming pool with diving boards and poolside chairlift for those with physical limitations.

Add to that the spectacular views from the highest point in southern Wisconsin, and you have all you need for a day of family fun.

Description and special features. In addition to the above mentioned features, 78 campsites, including facilities for the handicapped, are available. Among more than six miles of hiking trails are:

Flintrock Nature Trail, with some 30 informational stops identifying trees and plants along the way.

East Tower Trail, with a steep slope from the tower to the swimming pool.

Pleasure Valley Trail, which starts at the pool parking lot and goes through maple and oak woods. Wisconsin's tallest (88 feet) example of the slippery elm tree is near the trail.

Military Ridge State Trail also passes along the southern border of the park. (See pp. 97–98.)

Degree of difficulty. Because the park occupies a 1,716-foot-high hill, some trails slope steeply, but they are generally wide and well-maintained natural turf.

How to get there. The village of Blue Mounds is located in western Dane County just north of U.S. 18-151. Take Mounds Park Road north from the village to the park entrance.

When open. The year around. A state park admission sticker is

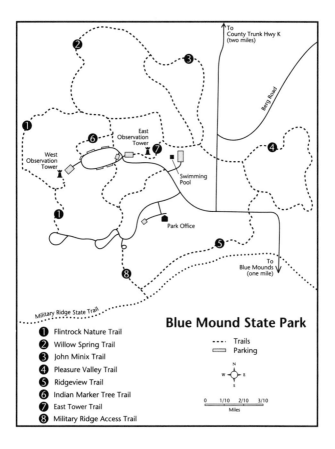

Blue Mound State Park

--- Trails

▭ Parking

1. Flintrock Nature Trail
2. Willow Spring Trail
3. John Minix Trail
4. Pleasure Valley Trail
5. Ridgeview Trail
6. Indian Marker Tree Trail
7. East Tower Trail
8. Military Ridge Access Trail

To County Trunk Hwy K (two miles)

Berg Road

East Observation Tower

West Observation Tower

Swimming Pool

Park Office

To Blue Mounds (one mile)

Military Ridge State Trail

N
W   E
S

0   1/10   2/10   3/10
Miles

required. The swimming pool is open from Memorial Day to Labor Day.

Facilities. Complete (see above).

Other points of interest in area

Noted for the variety and color of its formations, Cave of the Mounds is one of the most significant caves in the Upper Midwest. Open 9 A.M. to 5 P.M. daily, mid-March to Memorial Day and Labor Day to mid-November; 9 A.M. to 7 P.M. in summer; Saturday and Sunday in winter. A fee is charged. From Mount Horeb, go west on U.S. 18-151 for 3 miles, exit right on Cave of the Mounds Road to County PD, and follow the signs.

In the same area, Little Norway has authentically furnished log buildings of an 1856 homestead of Norwegian immigrants. It's open daily from May through October. A fee is charged.

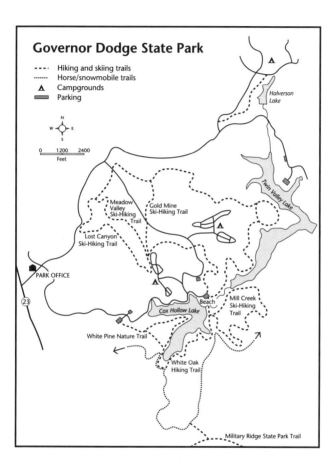

Governor Dodge State Park

- - - - Hiking and skiing trails
.... Horse/snowmobile trails
▲ Campgrounds
▬ Parking

N
W · E
S

0   1200   2400
Feet

Halverson
Lake

Twin Valley Lake

Meadow
Valley
Ski-Hiking
Trail

Gold Mine
Ski-Hiking Trail

Lost Canyon
Ski-Hiking Trail

PARK OFFICE

23

Mill Creek
Ski-Hiking
Trail

Beach

Cox Hollow Lake

White Pine Nature Trail

White Oak
Hiking Trail

Military Ridge State Park Trail

2 Hike up Steep Hills and into Deep Valleys in This Park

Governor Dodge State Park, Dodgeville

👟 👟 👟 👟

One of the few large state parks in the Driftless Area, where the great Ice Age glaciers did not go, provides hiking trails on steep hills and into narrow valleys.

No glaciers came to grind down the sheer bluffs of St. Peter's sandstone that was laid down on sea bottoms of the area 450 million years ago, nor did glaciers fill up the valleys. Park builders were able to create deep lakes for the fishing and swimming that contribute to the great popularity of Governor Dodge State Park.

Description and special features. Two trails are designated exclusively for hiking:

White Pine Nature Trail. Thirty-five informational labels provide facts and interpretation about the great variety of trees, shrubs, and animals in the area. While the hillside forests are basically of oaks, a large selection of other hardwoods and conifers on the two-mile trail are identified—ash, ironwood, bitternut, basswood, and maple, as well as white, red, and jack pine and red cedar. The hiker is treated to scenic views of Cox Hollow Lake from a ridge above it, and then the trail descends to the lakeside before returning to its trailhead at Enee Point.

White Oak Hiking Trail. Starting at the Cox Hollow Lake beach area, this 4.5-mile wooded trail crosses the earthen dam forming the lake and ascends the hills along its eastern shore, providing bird's-eye views of the lake. Around the south end of the lake it joins White Pine Nature Trail. You can either follow the loop of that trail and retrace your route to the beach or continue on to Enee Point and return to the beach area on Cox Hollow Road, a walk of about a mile.

Four trails are open both to hikers and cross-country skiers. Park literature provides the following descriptions of them:

Gold Mine Ski-Hiking Trail is a 2.5-mile loop. From the trailhead 0.4 mile west of the Twin Valley Campground entrance, the trail meanders through a variety of woods and meadows without encountering the steeper grades of other trails.

Mill Creek Ski-Hiking Trail is a 3.3-mile loop that begins in the Cox Hollow beach picnic area. Winding through meadows and wooded valleys, the trail also provides spectacular views of both Cox Hollow and Twin Valley lakes. You will encounter several steep grades, but most of the trail is quite level.

Meadow Valley Ski-Hiking Trail, a 6.8 mile loop, begins at Cox Hollow beach picnic area. More difficult than the Mill Creek Trail because of its length and steep grades, it follows along the ridge of the Lost Canyon and passes through open meadows and wooded ridges.

Lost Canyon Ski-Hiking Trail, an 8.1-mile loop, also starts at the Cox Hollow beach picnic area. With several steep grades, the trail is mostly wooded and passes through the scenic Lost Canyon, Stevens Falls, and Twin Lakes areas.

Degree of difficulty. Trails are well maintained, but many have steep grades. Earth-filled wood-beam stairs ascend the steepest slopes of the White Pine and White Oak trails.

How to get there. The park entrance is on State Highway 23, 3 miles north of U.S. 18.

When open. The year around from 6 A.M. to 11 P.M. except for overnight campers. A state park sticker is required.

Facilities. Governor Dodge is a full-service state park, including 267 individual campsites and additional group campsites. Rest rooms with showers are near the campgrounds. If you plan to do a lot of hiking, camp at the Cox Lake Campground, which is closer to most trails. The park also has two swimming beaches with bathhouses, numerous picnic areas with tables, grills and shelters, drinking water, and toilets. During the summer, concession stands offer snacks and pop. Canoes and rowboats may be rented on the two larger lakes, Cox Hollow and Twin Valley.

Other points of interest in area

The House on the Rock, 5 miles north of the park entrance on Highway 23, perches on a 450-foot-high rock outcropping. Expanded greatly over the years, this major attraction includes buildings that feature circuses and dolls, a millhouse, village shops, and a giant carousel. A fee is charged.

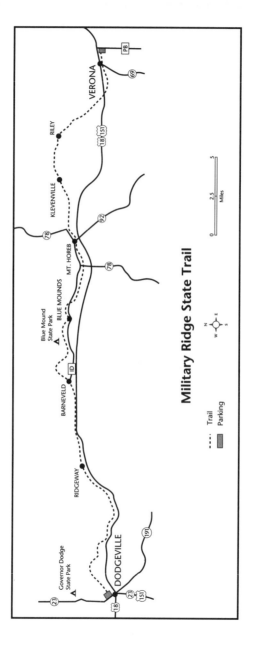

Military Ridge State Trail

Trail ·········
Parking ▭

3 State's First Highway Now a Multipurpose Trail

Military Ridge State Trail, southwestern Wisconsin

Picture yourself immersed in Wisconsin's early history as you follow part of the route of the state's first main highway, the Old Military Road. The road traversed hills, valleys, prairies, woodlands, and wetlands between strategic forts at Green Bay, Portage, and Prairie du Chien.

Built on an abandoned railroad bed, this trail traces the southwestern part of the Military Road through the Driftless Area atop a ridge separating major watersheds.

Description and special features. Starting just east of Verona near the junction of U.S. 18-151 and County PB, the trail passes through Verona, crosses the terminal moraine left by the continental glacier, and crosses the Sugar River valley near the unincorporated hamlet of Riley. Look for remnants of the presettlement prairie, with its many wildflowers.

After going through Mt. Horeb, a mecca for antique and craft item collectors, the trail joins the route of the Old Military Road. Passing the Cave of the Mounds, a commercial cave near the village of Blue Mounds, the trail goes through the village and along the southern border of Blue Mound State Park, which has camping facilities and a swimming pool.

It proceeds to Barneveld, the site of a devastating tornado that killed nine people in 1984. Trail builders recently completed a five-mile break in the trail between Barneveld and Ridgeway. From Ridgeway it continues on to Dodgeville, where it ends near Governor Dodge State Park.

Degree of difficulty. Open for both hiking and biking, as well as cross-country skiing and snowmobiling, the 40-mile trail is wide and mostly level with 48 sturdy bridges crossing creeks and rivers. Compacted limestone screenings make a firm but not too hard paving. If there is any disadvantage to this type of trail, it is that the route of the former railroad was selected for its easy grade rather than the most interesting terrain.

How to get there. You can enter the trail at any crossroad along the way. For convenience, park your car at either of the lots provided at each end of the trail, east of Verona on County PB, or just east of State Highway 23 in Dodgeville.

When open. From 6 A.M. to 11 P.M. the year around. Access for hikers is free. Daily fee for bicyclists is $1.50 for residents, $2.00 for nonresidents.

Facilities. To take full advantage of the trail's facilities and benefits, buy a copy of the 32-page booklet *History and Guide: Military Ridge State Park Trail,* for less than $2.00. Write Trail Manager, Governor Dodge State Park, Rte. 1, Dodgeville, WI 53533 (telephone 608-935-2315).

Other points of interest in area

Mt. Horeb has specialty boutiques and antique shops that sell Swedish crystal, Norwegian pewter, and Scandinavian jewelry and porcelain. The restored Hoff Mall has a variety of quaint shops and antique dealers' booths.

See Blue Mound State Park, pp. 89–91, and Governor Dodge State Park, pp. 93–95.

4 Trails Converge on Historic Shot Tower

Tower Hill State Park, Spring Green

Hikers on this park's trails get a glimpse of how shot for early nineteenth-century muzzle loader rifles was made. You'll see a shot tower that was constructed in the 1830s, abandoned in 1861, and reconstructed by the Department of Natural Resources in cooperation with the State Historical Society in 1971.

Description and special features. Several trails go from the picnic and camping areas of the park to the shot tower and shaft on three levels. One trail climbs to the top of a sandstone cliff and steep hill 180 feet above Mill Creek–Wisconsin River bottomlands. At the top of the hill is the reconstructed smelter house, where workers melted lead, laced it with arsenic, and dropped it through a sieve to form balls of lead.

A second trail goes to the tower shaft at an opening in the middle, at about 100 feet from the bottom. Continue on this trail following stone slab steps to the bottom of the shaft. Inside a 90-foot hand-dug tunnel workers caught the dropping lead globules in a basin of cold water, where the cooling process was completed. They then sorted the shot by size and shipped it on riverboats.

A trail from the mouth of the tunnel follows the base of the cliff to a ravine and gradually climbs a ridge to a gazebo built on the ridge's highest point. The trail then returns to the campground.

Degree of difficulty. Several trails have steep slopes. The trail to the middle of the shaft follows the very edge of the cliff, which is safely fenced off. The steeper trails are paved with blacktop or have stairs of stone slabs. Others are unpaved. Total distance of all trails is about 1.5 miles.

How to get there. On State Highway 23 about 2 miles south of Spring Green, just south of the Wisconsin River bridge, turn left onto County C, and go 1 mile to the park on the left.

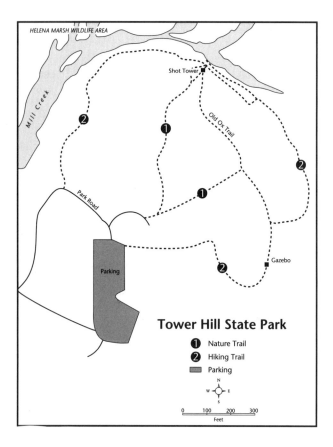

HELENA MARSH WILDLIFE AREA

Mill Creek

Shot Tower

Old Ox Trail

Park Road

Parking

Gazebo

Tower Hill State Park

1 Nature Trail
2 Hiking Trail
Parking

N
W E
S

0   100   200   300
Feet

When open. Tower Hill Park is officially open from May through October. You may walk trails at other times when there is no snow cover. A state park sticker is required. Park in the DNR office parking lot when the park is closed.

Facilities. Parking, picnic shelters including an enclosed shelter with fireplace, 15 primitive campsites, pit toilets, and playground. You may launch your canoe or boat from the park on Mill Creek about one-quarter mile before it empties into the Wisconsin River.

Other points of interest in area

The Springs Resort, with its cross-country ski trails and golf course, is on County C just west of the park entrance on the left.

Taliesin, a compound for architectural students, built by Frank Lloyd Wright and now operated by a foundation, offers tours from Memorial Day through mid-October. A fee is charged. From the junction of State Highway 23 and County C, go south on Highway 23 for about one mile.

Jefferson County

While you are walking you cannot be reached by telephone or telegraph, and you cannot reach anybody in those ways. That in itself is a great blessing.

Donald Culross Peattie, THE JOY OF WALKING

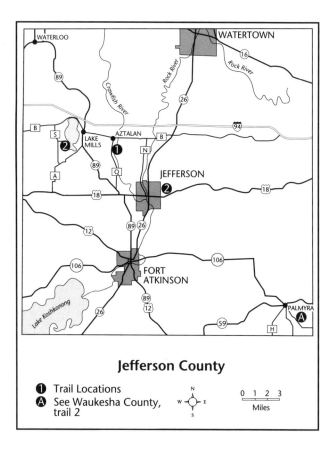

Jefferson County

1 Trail Locations
A See Waukesha County, trail 2

N
W—E
S

0 1 2 3
Miles

1 Were These Altars Used for Cannibalistic Rituals?

Aztalan State Park, Lake Mills

👟 👟

As you walk from the gate down toward the Crawfish River you may be following the torchbearers of an earlier ritualistic procession involving human sacrifice on one of the great altars of this place. Compared with Native Americans of surrounding areas, the Upper Mississippians of this enclave were advanced culturally, but probably also cannibalistic while their village flourished between A.D. 1100 and 1300.

Description and special features. Although this 172-acre park does contain hiking trails, we recommend you roam freely among the restored mounds and pyramids of its gently rolling, mowed surface. Sacrificial mounds and others of unknown purpose, as well as the corners of an original wooden palisade, have been reconstructed. The palisade surrounded a village of about 21 acres.

Degree of difficulty. Easy walking, with well-mowed surfaces and blacktop drives.

How to get there. From Lake Mills go 2 miles east on County B, then about a quarter mile south on County Q to the park entrance on the left.

When open. 7 A.M. to 9 P.M. April through November. State park admission sticker is not required.

Facilities. Parking, flush toilets, picnic tables and shelter, grills.

Other points of interest in area

Aztalan Museum, a former pioneer village just north of the park on County Q, has a church, an 1840s cabin, school, and artifacts of pioneer days. It is open May 15 through September 30. A small fee is charged.

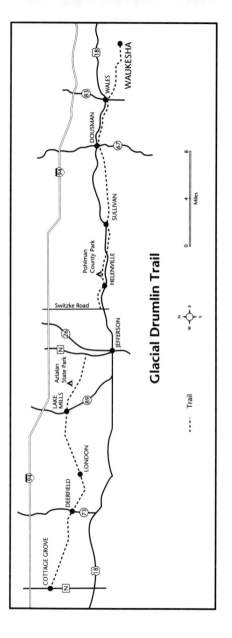

Glacial Drumlin Trail

WAUKESHA

WALES

(18)

(83)

DOUSMAN

(67)

(94)

SULLIVAN

Pohlman
County Park

HELENVILLE

Switzke Road

JEFFERSON

(26)

N

Aztalan
State Park

LAKE
MILLS

(89)

LONDON

(94)

DEERFIELD

(73)

COTTAGE GROVE

(18)

N

N
W   E
S

0   4   8
Miles

- - - -   Trail

2 Glacier Monuments That You Can Walk Among

Glacial Drumlin Trail, southern and southeastern Wisconsin

When the great Laurentide Ice Sheet occupied major portions of the northern hemisphere, until about 10,000 years ago, it literally transformed the land, grinding down hills and mountains, filling in valleys, and creating entirely new landforms in their place.

In Wisconsin, as well as in Minnesota and New York, the glacier left monuments of its passing called *drumlins,* a type of elongated or oval-shaped hill of unstratified earth and rocks called drift. The longer axes of these hills run parallel to the direction the glacier moved. The hills vary in height from a few feet to over 100 feet and are up to a quarter-mile wide and two miles long.

Some 1,400 drumlins pimple southeastern Wisconsin. The 47-mile Glacial Drumlin Trail runs east and west through the heart of the drumlin terrain between the village of Cottage Grove and the city of Waukesha.

Description and special features. The trail goes through Deerfield, London, Lake Mills, Helenville, Sullivan, Dousman, and Wales. There is a four-mile break just northeast of Jefferson. Nearly every town has grocery stores and restaurants.

The trail is open for hiking, biking, cross-country skiing, and snowmobiling. A folder giving details about the trail route is available from vendors along the way, from east and west section headquarters, or by writing to Lake Kegonsa Work Unit, 2405 Door Creek Road, Stoughton, WI 53589 (telephone 608-873-9695), or Lapham Peak Unit—KMSF, N846-W329 CTH "C", Delafield, WI 53018 (telephone 414-646-3025).

Bicyclists over 18 must buy nominally priced admission cards, either at one of the above addresses, from a ranger along the trail, or from vendors in town.

Degree of difficulty. Following an abandoned railroad bed, the trail never has more than a 3 percent grade. Limestone screenings provide a firm, but not-too-hard, surface.

How to get there. The western portion of the trail begins just across from the post office at County N in Cottage Grove and ends at County N north of Jefferson. The trail resumes with the eastern portion at Switzke Road east of Jefferson and ends at MacArthur Road about one-quarter mile west of St. Paul Avenue on the west side of Waukesha.

When open. From 6 A.M. to 11 P.M. the year around.

Facilities. There are parking lots on each end and in Deerfield, Lake Mills, Sullivan, Dousman, and Wales.

Other points of interest in area

See Aztalan State Park, p. 105, and the Kettle Moraine State Forest, pp. 203–9.

Kenosha County

For a naturalist, the most productive pace is a snail's pace. A large part of his walk is often spent standing still. A mile an hour may well be fast enough.

Edwin Way Teale, WALKING DOWN A RIVER

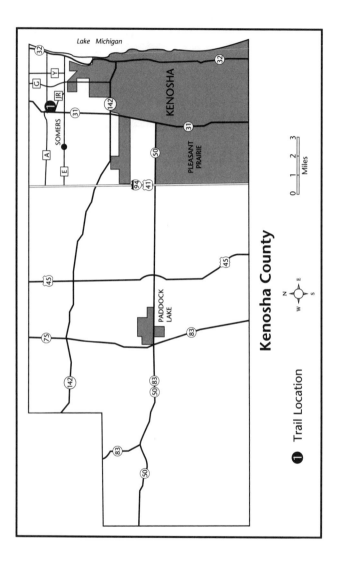

Kenosha County

Lake Michigan

KENOSHA

PLEASANT PRAIRIE

SOMERS

PADDOCK LAKE

N
W · E
S

0 1 2 3
Miles

● Trail Location

1 River Valley Park Provides Scenic Setting for Trails

Petrifying Springs Park, northeastern Kenosha County

Springs seeping through limestone coat surrounding rocks and twigs grey, giving them a petrified look. That's how this 360-acre county park in the valley of the Pike River got its name. The oldest park under Kenosha County jurisdiction, Petrifying Springs was developed during the 1930s. Continuing improvement and attention have resulted in a well-maintained mutli-use park that contains not only a network of trails but also an 18-hole golf course and lots of picnic and playground areas.

Description and special features. Hiking trails lace approximately 75 acres of mature hardwood forest. At several points they connect to limestone-covered paths in open areas.

A trail in the best hiking area, a 30-acre wooded preserve north of County A, follows the rim of a ravine through which the river flows. Hikers can get a bird's-eye view of the river from the trail along the rim as it descends toward the river. The trail then doubles back along the riverbank.

The Indian Springs Trail crosses the river from an open area and goes by several springs seeping from the hillside. A plaque marks the location of the cabin of Kenosha County's first settler.

Degree of difficulty. Trails vary in width and slope. Wood chips pave heavily used trails in forested areas. The park has built several sturdy bridges across the river connecting trails to open areas.

How to get there. From State Highway 31 take County JR east about one-half mile to an entrance on the left. Farther north from 31 take County A to entrances right or left. Only the entrance from JR is open on weekends during the summer.

When open. From sunrise to 10 P.M. the year around. A small fee is charged on weekends from May 1 through Labor Day.

Facilities. In addition to ample parking and the golf course, there are rest rooms, large open picnic areas with shelters, softball diamonds, equipped playgrounds, and concession stands. Cross-country ski trails and a sledding hill are available in winter.

Other points of interest in area

Bristol Woods Park, a mostly undeveloped 198-acre county park, has wooded trails for the hiker seeking quieter surroundings. It has a picnic shelter. Location is just south of the intersection of County C and MB, about two miles west of I-94.

Bong State Recreation Area, in the northwestern portion of the county, is a 4,500-acre multi-use area with 14 miles of hiking trails through woods and grasslands. It has two self-guided nature trails; facilities for picnicking, camping, hunting, and many special uses; and a 130-acre lake and swimming beach. Bong is located on State Highway 142 17 miles west of Kenosha and 6 miles east of Burlington.

Milwaukee County

One of the shining moments of my day is that when, having returned a little weary from an afternoon walk, I exchange boots for slippers, out-of-doors coat for easy, familiar, shabby jacket, and, in my deep, soft elbowed chair, await the tea-tray.

George Gissing, THE PRIVATE PAPERS OF HENRY RYECROFT

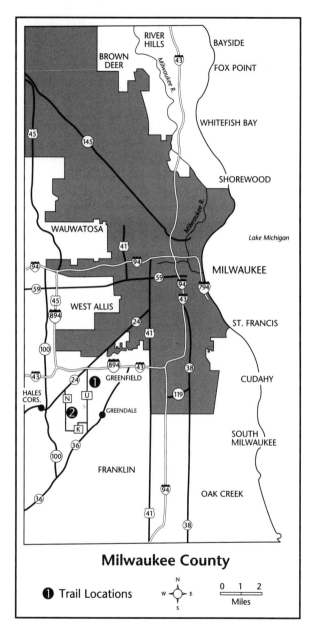

Milwaukee County

● Trail Locations

N
W — E
S

0 1 2
Miles

1 Mall and Medical Center Encourage Walkers

Southridge Mall, Milwaukee

Mall walking is alive and well in Milwaukee. While none of the shopping malls I contacted discouraged walkers, management's attitude toward walkers ranged from eager support to benign neglect. Southridge Mall likes its walkers a lot and encourages them in a variety of ways.

"We publish an occasional newsletter for walkers called 'The Walkers' Beat,'" says Joni Vasos, marketing director. In conjunction with St. Luke's Medical Center's Freedom 55–65 program, the mall also makes available blood pressure screening from 7:45 to 8:45 A.M. Tuesdays and Thursdays. In addition, St. Luke's sponsors a Mall Walkers Wellness Event one day in October, with booths providing information on health topics. The mall also has arranged with over a dozen of its stores to offer discounts to senior citizens.

Description and special features. Southridge is a two-level indoor shopping mall. Following the perimeter of the indoor common area on either the lower or upper level, the distance is about one-half mile.

Degree of difficulty. The climate control of an indoor mall makes it easy to walk despite blizzard or thunderstorm outside. Wear well-cushioned shoes for the hard surface.

How to get there. Southridge Mall is located at 5300 South 76th Street (County U), which is several blocks south of I-43.

When open. For walkers, doors open at 6:30 A.M. daily except Easter, Thanksgiving, and Christmas. The mall closes at 6 P.M. Saturday, 5 P.M. Sunday, and 9 P.M. weekdays.

Facilities. Parking, rest rooms on each floor, and a variety of restaurants in the Greenridge Cafes area and elsewhere.

115

Other points of interest in area

Other major indoor malls in the Milwaukee area are North-ridge, 7700 West Brown Deer Road; Mayfair, 2500 Mayfair Road; Brookfield Square, Moorland Road just north of I-94; Southgate Mall, 3333 South 27th Street; Grand Avenue, 275 West Wisconsin Avenue; Bay Shore, 5900 North Port Washington Road; and Capitol Court, 5500 West Capitol Drive.

2 Four Walking Places Satisfy a Variety of Interests

Whitnall Park, Hales Corners

Do you like to walk among cultivated flowers, in a nature preserve, through a hardwood forest, or along a parkway? Take your pick at Whitnall Park and adjoining areas in Milwaukee County.

Description and special features. Four walking areas are in or adjacent to the 600-acre park.

Boerner Botanical Gardens was designed as an English country garden by Alfred L. Boerner and developed starting in 1932. A showplace for plants, flowers, and apple trees, the garden's asphalt-paved walkways meander among hundreds of varieties, each clearly labeled. A Bog Garden Walk, on an elevated boardwalk, is one of the many highlights of Boerner. These walkways are strictly for strollers who prefer to pause and enjoy. Different varieties of perennials and annuals blossom from April through October.

Wehr Nature Center has hiking and nature trails through woods, across meadows, and around a large pond. While Boerner displays cultivated plants, Wehr is dedicated to preserving and interpreting native plant and animal communities. Trails mostly paved with wood chips make walking easy. Stop at Wehr Nature Center for a copy of its newsletter, which tells about the many organized programs held there.

Milton C. Potter School Forest, locally known as *Potter's Woods,* is adjacent to the botanical gardens. You may enter the mature hardwood forest from the north side of the gardens. Originally designed as a nature trail, it no longer provides an identification guide to plants and trees. But the wide, unpaved trail through the forest offers a quiet setting for walkers preferring seclusion.

Root River Parkway runs along the Root River northeast of Whitnall from 92nd Street to Forest Home Avenue. Trails on each side of the river are not well maintained, but you can walk

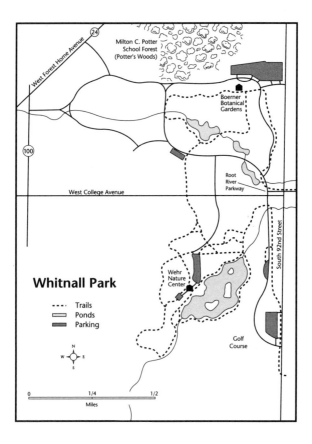

Milton C. Potter
School Forest
(Potter's Woods)

West Forest Home Avenue

24

100

West College Avenue

Boerner Botanical Gardens

Root River Parkway

South 92nd Street

Whitnall Park

- - - - Trails
Ponds
Parking

Wehr
Nature
Center

Golf
Course

N
W   E
S

0   1/4   1/2
Miles

or jog the mowed grassy areas along the river and the Parkway's drive. Picnic areas, with tables and rest rooms, dot the parkway.

Degree of difficulty. All trails within Whitnall and Potter's Woods are well maintained and easy to walk.

How to get there. Whitnall is located at 5879 South 92nd Street between Grange and Rawson Avenues south of I-894-43. Take the 84th or 76th Street exit and follow Forest Home Avenue (State Highway 24) southwest to a left turn onto 92nd Street.

When open. Boerner Gardens are open 8 A.M. to sunset daily April through October. Wehr, Potter's Woods, and Root River Parkway are open the year around for walking but are not maintained in winter.

Facilities. Parking, rest rooms. Root River Parkway has picnic facilities.

Other points of interest in area

Experience a tropical jungle, an African desert, and a themed floral garden all in one visit at the Mitchell Park Horticultural Conservatory, 524 South Layton Boulevard, Milwaukee 53215. Three climate-controlled domes—Tropical, Arid, and Show—contain more than 1,200 plant species from five continents.

Ozaukee County

We walk in order to enjoy what the road has to offer. We ride in order to get quickly to the inn.

Joseph Wood Krutch, Is Walking the New Status Symbol?

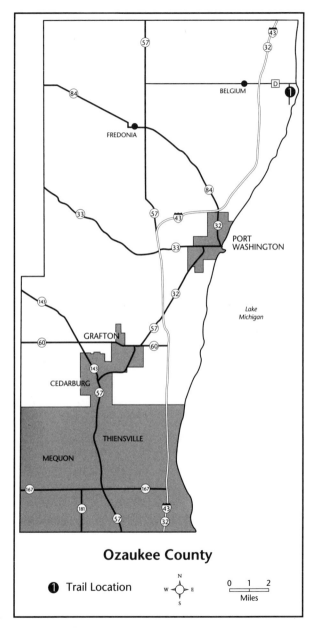

Ozaukee County

① Trail Location

0 1 2
Miles

1 Walk a Beach, around a Quarry, or through a Cedar Forest

Harrington Beach State Park, Belgium

👟 👟 👟

Nature and the effects of human activity have made this 637-acre park unique in its variety of trails. Nature provides a sandy, pebble-strewn beach and a lakeshore forest, while a century-old quarry, now filled with water, provides a clear, deep lake that's rimmed with a scenic trail. Only 35 miles from Milwaukee, the park is a quiet place to walk except during hot summer weekends when swimmers and sunbathers flock to its Lake Michigan beach.

Description and special features. A beach and two trails provide three distinctly different walking experiences. If you enjoy the sounds of waves from an inland, fresh-water sea and the sight of gulls and sandpipers, stroll along the mile-long beach.

Quarry Lake Trail hugs the rim of an old limestone quarry and provides serene views through the cedars of the blue 26-acre lake and stone ledges rising above the water.

The one-half-mile *White Cedar Swamp Trail* will take you through a lowland forest of cedars, birches, maples, and aspens. It's a self-guided nature trail with informational stops describing this remnant of a type of forest that was once typical of the cool lakeshore environment.

Degree of difficulty. Except for one built-up dune in its center, the beach is flat and wide with a firm surface. The Quarry Lake Trail has gentle undulations and often goes to the very edge of the quarry walls, but hikers are protected in most such places by a split-rail fence. Sturdy bridges cross a small stream in several places. The White Cedar Swamp Trail is flat and wide. Portions of it may be soggy in wet weather.

How to get there. From the intersection of I-43 and County D just east of Belgium, go east on County D for 1 mile to the park entrance on the right.

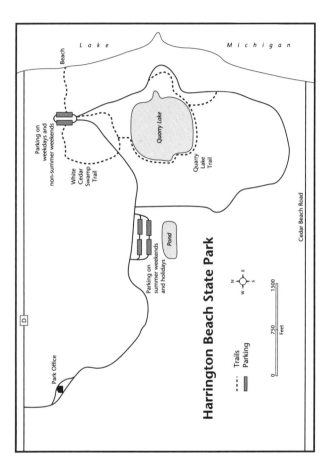

Harrington Beach State Park

Lake **Michigan**

Beach

Parking on
weekdays and
non-summer weekends

White
Cedar
Swamp
Trail

Quarry Lake

Quarry
Lake
Trail

Pond

Parking on
summer weekends
and holidays

Cedar Beach Road

Park Office

D

N
W E
S

Trails
Parking

0   750   1500
Feet

When open. The year around from 6 A.M. to 11 P.M. for this day-use park. A state park sticker is required.

Facilities. This well-equipped state park has seven designated picnic areas with about 100 tables, grills, and drinking water; three picnic shelters; year-round pit toilets; two volleyball courts and two horseshoe courts. You can fish in Quarry Lake and in an additional pond, Puckett Lake, which is stocked with trout.

During summer weekends a bus shuttles between the upper parking lot and the beach area. During other times you may drive to a lot near the beach.

Other points of interest in area

The Ozaukee County Historical Society's Pioneer Village, a living museum of restored log, half-timber, and other buildings from throughout the county, is at the north edge of Hawthorne Hills Park. Located about 2 miles southwest of Fredonia on County I, the village is open Wednesdays, Saturdays, and Sundays from Memorial Day to Labor Day, and Saturdays and Sundays only until the second Sunday in October. A fee is charged.

Racine County

You would be astonished if I were to tell you all the grave and learned heads who have confessed to me that, when on walking tours, they sang.

Robert Louis Stevenson, WALKING TOURS

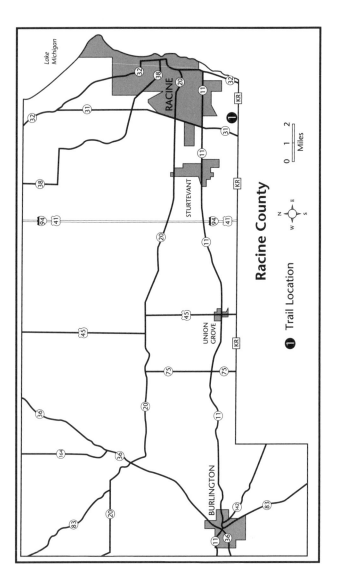

Racine County

Lake Michigan

RACINE

STURTEVANT

UNION
GROVE

BURLINGTON

N
W   E
S

0   1   2
Miles

● 1   Trail Location

1 Trail Meanders through State Scientific Area

Sanders Park, southeastern Racine County

👟 👟

A 30-acre State of Wisconsin Designated Scientific Area of hardwoods and wildflowers is the setting for the trails in this park. Set aside as an example of presettlement forest, the preserve contains several varieties of large old oak trees with hickories, maples, and other hardwoods sprinkled in. More than 90 kinds of native wildflowers also grow there.

Description and special features. The trail meanders through the forest, which is surrounded by open areas, and follows a small brook for a portion of its length. The forest can be entered from each of the open areas via trail spurs. Total distance is about 1.5 miles.

A one-mile jogging trail with an asphalt surface also loops through the park.

Degree of difficulty. The terrain is mostly flat and the hiking trail is unmarked but easy to follow. During my springtime walk there, I noticed that mountain bikes had put ruts in some moist portions of the natural turf.

How to get there. From State Highway 31, at the Racine-Kenosha county line, go east on County KR for 1 mile, then north on Wood Road for 0.4 mile to the park entrance on the right.

When open. Sunrise to sunset the year around. Camping and picnicking facilities are available from April to October.

Facilities. In addition to parking, the park offers more than 30 individual campsites (most with electricity); comfort station with showers; and a recreational vehicle dump station. For picnicking the park has tables and grills, an architecturally designed shelter with a cooking hearth, electricity, and drinking water.

The 80-acre park also has pit toilets, a baseball diamond, a horseshoe court, and children's play equipment.

Other points of interest in area

Architect Frank Lloyd Wright designed the S. C. Johnson Wax Administration Center, the company's international headquarters. Its unique features include slim dendriform columns supporting the roof and glass tubing instead of windows in the Great Workroom. Located at the corner of Fourteenth and Franklin streets, the building may be toured Tuesday through Sunday in summer and Tuesday through Friday other times (call 414-631-2154 for reservations).

Rock County

All walking is discovery. On foot we take the time to see things whole. We see trees as well as forests, people as well as crowds.
Hal Borland, TO OWN THE STREETS AND FIELDS

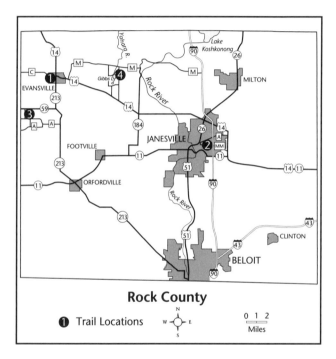

Rock County

● Trail Locations

N
W · E
S

0 1 2
Miles

1 Tour a Treasury of Preserved Architecture

Evansville Historic District

The Evansville Historic District in designed for strolling. Originally settled in the 1840s by New Englanders who came by way of Indiana, the town enjoyed post–Civil War prosperity based on an economy that provided support for farmers and lumbering interests. Townspeople who built homes especially from the 1860s to World War I chose a varied array of classical, revival, and other architectural styles.

It's remarkable that these homes avoided the wrecking ball and withstood the onslaught of gas stations and franchise restaurants that has reshaped similar small towns. Local historians attribute this to the slow, uneventful growth of Evansville and the recognition in recent decades by some citizens with unusual foresight that the homes were a unique resource well worth preserving. Through their efforts a 22-block section, representing a major portion of the city, was placed on the National Register of Historic Places in 1978.

Description and special features. Starting at Madison Street, walk west on Church Street for three-and-a-fraction blocks to College Drive. Go right, around a circular drive, to Fourth Street and right again to West Main Street. Go east on West Main Street for three blocks to First Street. Go left a couple of short blocks to view several houses and retrace your route on First Street. Resume walking east to Madison Street to view several houses within the blocks both right and left.

A few architectural highlights:

The Eager Free Public Library, 39 West Main Street, an example of Prairie School architecture built in 1908.

A Late Picturesque home, 44 West Main Street, with intersecting gable roof, corner tower, and projecting rounded front bay with curved glass.

A Queen Anne home, 114 West Main Street, with gables feature Palladian and arched leaded windows.

An 1879 Italianate home, 143 West Main Street, with carpenter's detailing such as denticulated cornice, punched and

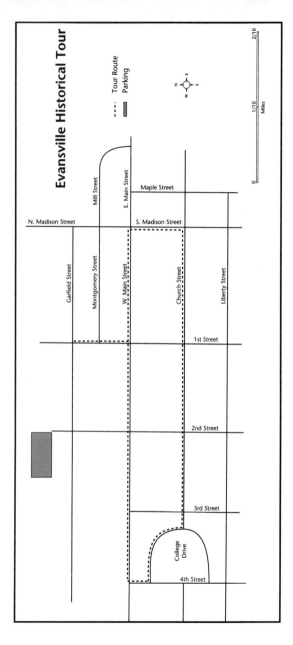

Evansville Historical Tour

Tour Route (dashed line)

Parking (shaded box)

N E
W S

Miles
0   1/10   2/10

Mill Street

E. Main Street

Maple Street

N. Madison Street

S. Madison Street

Garfield Street

Montgomery Street

W. Main Street

Church Street

Liberty Street

1st Street

2nd Street

3rd Street

College Drive

4th Street

hooded lintels over windows, and a bracketed entrance portico.

I strongly recommend the Historical and Architectural Walking Tour brochure, which locates and describes 48 homes and buildings. You can pick up a copy at the Antique Mall of Evansville, 13 West Main Street, as well as at other local businesses, or by writing to Evansville City Hall, 31 South Madison Street, Evansville, WI 53536.

Degree of difficulty. Level and easy one-mile walk, with residential streets and well-maintained concrete sidewalks.

How to get there. Evansville is 23 miles south of Madison and 20 miles west of Janesville on U.S. 14.

When open. Obviously, daylight hours are best for this walking tour. You may view an 18-minute slide show about the city and the Historical District anytime at the Antique Mall of Evansville (mentioned above), which is open from 10 A.M. to 5 P.M. daily except major holidays and from 12 noon to 4 P.M. Sundays.

Facilities. None.

Other points of interest in area

About 20 miles west of Evansville, the quaint town of New Glarus, settled by Swiss immigrants in 1845, has retained the traditional national architecture. You can feast on fondue and other authentic Swiss cuisine at the New Glarus Hotel and other local restaurants. Visit a historical museum or a lace factory. The 23-mile Sugar River Bike Trail also begins in the village. See pp. 83–86.

From Evansville take County C through Monticello and State Highway 69 north to New Glarus.

See also Brooklyn Wildlife Area Trail, p. 57.

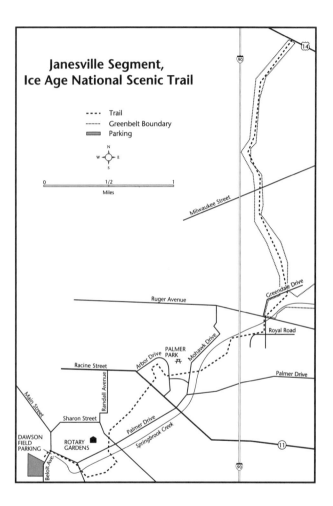

Janesville Segment,
Ice Age National Scenic Trail

- - - - Trail
.... Greenbelt Boundary
▭ Parking

N
W — E
S

0   1/2   1
                Miles

14

90

Greendale Drive

Milwaukee Street

Ruger Avenue

Royal Road

PALMER
PARK
⛩

Arbor Drive

Mohawk Drive

Palmer Drive

Racine Street

Randall Avenue

Main Street

Sharon Street

Palmer Drive

Springbrook Creek

DAWSON
FIELD
PARKING

ROTARY
GARDENS

Beloit Ave.

11

90

2 Trail Follows Bed of Glacial River Channel

Janesville Segment, Ice Age National Scenic Trail

👟 👟

Cascading meltwater of the great Laurentide Ice Sheet cut wide, branching ravines into an area that is now the northeast side of Janesville. You can follow that channel, a segment of the Ice Age Trail, through Janesville's greenbelt system.

Description and special features. At first following a usually dry creek literally paved with glacial rocks and stones, the trail goes into the ravine for 2.4 miles. Fine homes line the rim of the ravine on both sides. Natural prairie flora grow on the ancient channel bed.

The southern segment of the trail, 2.9 miles in length to be certified as part of the Ice Age Trail, generally follows Springbrook Creek through parks and bottomlands.

A third segment follows the west bank of the Rock River to Riverside Park in northwest Janesville. From the north end of the park a half-mile loop goes along a high bluff and down steep steps on the bluff, known as Devil's Staircase. It loops back to its starting point in the park, the north pavilion.

In one of the more ambitious southern Wisconsin trail-building projects of the Ice Age Trail organization, the northeast end of this trail system will someday be connected by an additional trail, partway over an old railroad bed, to the Kettle Moraine trail system near Whitewater. The northwest end will eventually connect with the Sugar River Trail in Brodhead.

Trail sponsors helped build and now maintain the trails. They include the local Jaycees, the Kiwanis Club, ANR Pipeline Co., the Bell Telephone Pioneers, the Wisconsin Conservation Corps, and the Janesville Parks Department.

Degree of difficulty. The Greenbelt segment is wide, mowed natural turf with a gentle incline that is easy to walk except over elevated roads crossing the ravine.

The south segment, though not well marked, is an easily walked path that follows parklands on either side of Palmer Drive. A portion loops through bottomlands of Springbrook

Creek, following an abandoned railroad bed for a while. Paving of this portion is compacted limestone screenings.

The Rock River segment, which goes northeast from the city's business district, also follows the west bank of the river. The Devil's Staircase loop, because of its steepness, was designed more for the physically fit hiker, according to Tom Presny, Janesville's park director.

How to get there. Enter the northern portion from the corner of Ruger Avenue and Greendale Drive. The trailhead is located directly across from the Janesville Community Day Care Center at 3103 Ruger Avenue on the city's east side. Park on the street.

You can enter the southern portion at the Dawson Ballfield Complex, 920 Beloit Avenue. Offstreet parking is available nearby.

You may park where you enter the Rock River segment on the west side of the river between Milwaukee Street and Centerway. This portion will eventually be joined to the southern segment, according to Presny.

When open. The year around. You may cross-country ski the northern and southern segments.

Facilities. The northern portion has no facilities. The southern and Rock River portions are served by facilities of the parks, including parking, picnic tables, grills, playground equipment, and rest rooms, which are available during the summer.

Other points of interest in area

Right on the trail, the Rotary Gardens near the corner of Palmer Drive and Sharon Street include a restored visitor center for both the gardens and the Ice Age National Scenic Trail, as well as the Jaycees Plant and Wildlife Refuge. Used for environmental education, the botanical garden has a colorful walkway and a trout pond. The gardens are open and free the year-around.

The Tallman Restorations, a villa built in 1857, at 440 North Jackson Street, includes many of the household conveniences of the day. For example, a storage tank in the attic, rather than the typical hand pump, supplied running water. Abraham Lincoln spent a weekend there in 1859. Open Tuesday through Sunday in summer and weekends May and September.

General Motors Assembly Plant, 1000 Industrial Avenue, is open all year except the week of Christmas and during model changes. Tours are at 9:30 A.M. and 1 P.M. Monday through Thursday.

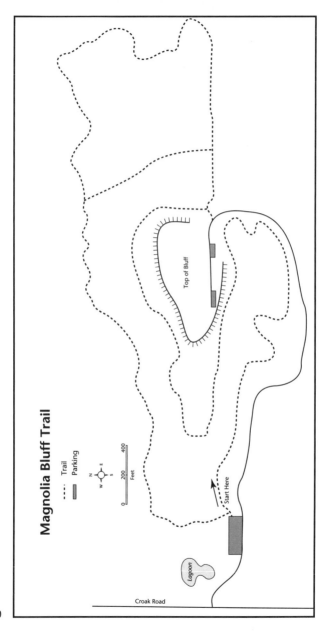

Magnolia Bluff Trail

Trail - - - -
Parking ▬▬

N
W · E
S

0   200   400
Feet

Top of Bluff

Start Here

Lagoon

Croak Road

3 Climb through Micro-Climates to Get Bluff-Top View

Magnolia Bluff County Park, northwestern Rock County

If you like a hilly, strenuous walking place, you'll love the trails in this 120-acre park. Climb a Driftless Area bluff and enjoy a spectacular view of surrounding farmland.

Description and special features. Its sheer walls facing north and south, the bluff harbors micro-climates that produce a diversity of plant life. The 2.9-mile trail starts near the parking lot and crisscrosses the south side of the bluff through mostly oaks and other hardwoods during its ascension. This portion of the itinerary offers a detailed view of sandstone outcroppings along the bluff's wall.

At the top of the bluff you'll enjoy not only an excellent view but also a pleasant picnic grounds.

The trail then comes down the north side through the county's only natural stand of white birch trees.

Walkers are also permitted on a 2.7-mile bridle path.

Degree of difficulty. The trail is narrow, sometimes steep, and often rocky. While it is also used for cross-country skiing, its slopes would make the going very difficult. If you want to enjoy the view but do not want to endure the climb, you may drive to the top on a paved road, which is open during the summer.

How to get there. From Evansville, go southwest on State Highway 59 for about 5 miles, then south on Croak Road for about a mile to the park, which is on the left.

When open. Rock County parks are open from 5 A.M. to 10 P.M. the year around. Hiking is not permitted during cross-country skiing season.

Facilities. There are parking, picnic tables, drinking water, and pit toilets at this rural location.

Other points of interest in area

See Evansville Historical District, pp. 133–35.

4 Glacier-formed Lake Provides Setting for Trail

Gibbs Lake County Park

A glacier-formed lake just north of the terminal moraine that runs through Rock County provides the setting for this lakeside trail. The rural location of the 299-acre park in the northwest section of the county ensures a quiet walk during most of the year.

Description and special features. Starting from the picnic area near the parking lot, the trail proceeds along the east side of the lake through low native vegetation and some hardwoods. At the south end of the lake it turns east and loops back through a prairie higher above the lake.

Cross-country skiers use the trail in season. Hikers may use a separate equestrian trail.

Degree of difficulty. Widely mowed natural turf of a path over fairly gentle slopes makes for easy walking. Lower portions of the trail may be muddy during wet weather.

How to get there. About a mile south of Fulton in northwestern Rock County, Gibbs Lake Road goes west from State Highway 184. Follow it several miles to the park on the left.

When open. Rock County parks are open from 5 A.M. to 10 P.M. daily.

Facilities. The park has a large parking lot, pit toilets, picnic tables, drinking water, and a boat launch.

Other points of interest in area

About 3 miles northeast of Gibbs Lake at the intersection of State Highway 184 and County M is Fulton. Before white pioneers arrived, Winnebago Indians grew corn nearby at the mouth of the Yahara River. The flatlands were known as Indian

Gardens and are still a fertile site for finding arrowheads among the large collection of Indian mounds.

Fulton Church in the village was organized in 1851 and is listed on the National Historic Register as the third oldest church in Rock County. Just north of Fulton on both sides of Highway 184, serene Murwin Park on the bank of the Yahara is ideal for fishing and riverside picnicking.

About two miles east on M, Indianford, so named because Indians used to ford the Rock River here, also has a little park where fishing is said to be very good near the Indianford dam.

Sauk County

In walking, the will and muscles are so accustomed to work together and perform their task with so little expenditure of force, that the intellect is left comparatively free.

Oliver Wendell Holmes, THE PLEASURE OF WALKING

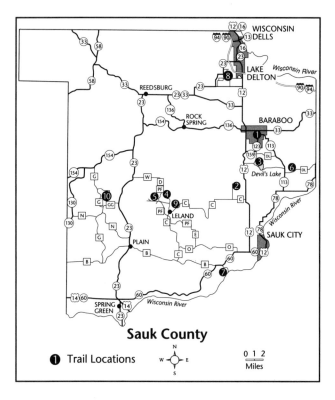

Sauk County

● Trail Locations

N
W ✦ E
S

0 1 2
Miles

1 "The Greatest Show on Earth" Was Born Here

Baraboo Historic Tour

When five sons of harnessmaker August Ringling staged their first Ringling Brothers Classic Comic and Concert Company in 1882, even their dreams did not include "The Greatest Show on Earth." But within two decades that's what it was called. Ringling Brothers Circus regaled "children of all ages" from coast to coast.

City fathers have authorized the publication of a walking tour brochure that provides the location and history of such places as the sites of the first tent show and the Al Ringling home, as well as other prominent historical buildings.

Description and special features. The tour described in the brochure is compact, with 25 sites centered on the Sauk County Courthouse in the middle of the town square. Ambitious walkers will also want to take in the 50-acre Circus World Museum (worth a day's visit in itself), where live circus acts are staged during the tourist season. Also within walking distance are the City Zoo, an unusually well-stocked and maintained facility for a city of 9,000, the Sauk County Historical Museum, and other places mentioned in the brochure.

You can obtain a free copy of the brochure by writing city hall at 135 Fourth Street, Baraboo, WI 53913. The Baraboo Area Chamber of Commerce will provide information about the Circus World Museum and other points on interest. The Chamber's address is 124 Second Street, Baraboo, WI 53913 (telephone 608- 356-8333).

Degree of difficulty. The walking tour described in the brochure is on well-maintained city sidewalks.

How to get there. Baraboo is located on U.S. 12 about 8 miles south of its junction with I-90–94 (exit 92).

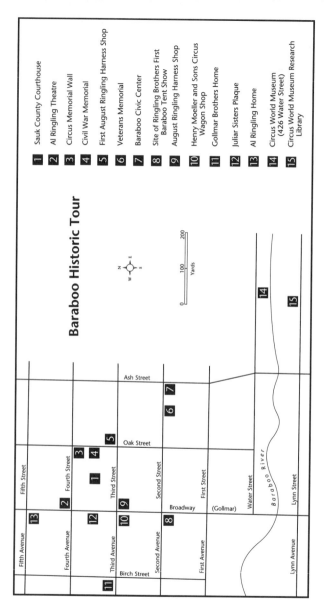

Baraboo Historic Tour

1 Sauk County Courthouse
2 Al Ringling Theatre
3 Circus Memorial Wall
4 Civil War Memorial
5 First August Ringling Harness Shop
6 Veterans Memorial
7 Baraboo Civic Center
8 Site of Ringling Brothers First Baraboo Tent Show
9 August Ringling Harness Shop
10 Henry Moeller and Sons Circus Wagon Shop
11 Gollmar Brothers Home
12 Juliar Sisters Plaque
13 Al Ringling Home
14 Circus World Museum (426 Water Street)
15 Circus World Museum Research Library

When open. While you can take the walking tour anytime during the year, the Circus World Museum is open from spring to late fall, with circus acts following a shorter summer season to about mid-September.

Facilities. The courthouse has public rest rooms.

Other points of interest in area

The Man Mound, located in Man Mound Park, is an Indian mound of a giant man with what appear to be wings protruding from his head. With a length of 214 feet and a width of 48 feet at the shoulders, it is the most prominent archaeological feature in the area. From Baraboo, go east on State Highway 33 for about a mile, then north on Rocky Point Road for a mile, then east on Man Mound Road for a mile to the park on the right.

Mid-Continent Railway and Museum. One-half mile west of the four-way stop in North Freedom, a small town west of Baraboo, the historical railway offers daily rides on old steam-driven trains. Trains depart for an hour's ride at 10:30 A.M. and 12:30, 2, and 3:30 P.M. from mid-May to Labor Day and weekends until mid-October. Train rides feature spectacular autumn colors the first two full weekends in October and a snow ride the third full weekend in February. A museum, open from 9:30 A.M. to 5 P.M., displays railroading artifacts. Fares are charged.

Devil's Lake State Park. See pp. 153–57 for details of this popular hiking place and for more information about points of interest in the area.

2 Hike through 2,900 Acres of Preserved Wilds

Baxter's Hollow

A walk along this primitive trail reveals a treasury of wild things preserved by the Wisconsin chapter of The Nature Conservancy.

Description and special features. After approaching the preserve through the picturesque gorge formed by Otter Creek, park at one of several spaces along the road and hike in on an unpaved path. It crosses native prairie, creek and woods, past the old Klondike Campground, and into the quartzite bluffs.

The 2,900-acre preserve is the Conservancy's largest in Baraboo Hills and the most diverse in its protected species. Some 135 kinds of birds have been identified there, as well as the pickerel frog and other examples of rare aquatic life. Both southern and northern tree types inhabit the Otter Creek watershed. A hike into the solitude of the hollow brings to mind the spirits of the Paleo-Indians that inhabited the place some 10,000 postglacial years ago.

Degree of difficulty. Wear durable hiking shoes. While most of the path ascends slowly, it is narrow and crosses the creek without the benefit of a bridge. To avoid damaging rare plants, do not stray off the trail.

How to get there. From U.S. 12, midway between Sauk City and Baraboo, go west on County C for 1.5 miles, then north on Stone Pocket Road for about 2 miles into the wooded gorge. There are several turn-off parking spaces.

When open. The year around. Path may be impassable in winter.

Facilities. None.

Other points of interest in area

See Parfrey's Glen, pp. 162–65, and Hemlock Draw, pp. 158–59, also in the Baraboo Hills.

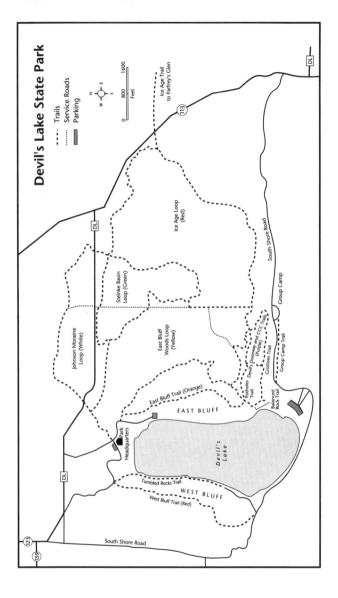

Devil's Lake State Park

Trails
Service Roads
Parking

N
W E
S

0 800 1600
Feet

Ice Age Trail
to Parfrey's Glen

113

DL

Ice Age Loop
(Red)

Steinke Basin
Loop (Green)

Johnson Moraine
Loop (White)

East Bluff
Woods Loop
(Yellow)

South Shore Road

Group Camp

Group Camp Trail

Potholes Trail

Devil's Doorway and CCC Trail
(Purple)

Grottoes Trail

Balanced Rock Trail

East Bluff Trail (Orange)

EAST BLUFF

Park Headquarters

Devil's Lake

Tumbled Rocks Trail

WEST BLUFF

West Bluff Trail (Red)

DL

123

15

South Shore Road

152

3 More than a Million Enjoy These Trails Each Year

Devil's Lake State Park, Baraboo

There's a legend that two suitors, a Frenchman and an Indian brave, dearly loved the beautiful Indian maiden Minnewawa, who lived in a village near Devil's Lake. They fought each other over her and both men died. After hearing of this Minnewawa took her own life. It could be said the men in Minnewawa's life loved her to death.

The legend lives today at the lake, but with a different twist. The lake and its rocky scenery are like Minnewawa. She's loved so much by her "suitors" that their vast numbers would love her to death if it weren't for park managers' constant vigilance. Devil's Lake's facilities have endured many more than one million users each year since 1952.

Devil's Lake has everything an individual walker or family could want: hiking trails that show off the area's breathtaking views, roomy campsites, sandy beaches, clear water for swimming, scuba diving or fishing, plenty of picnic shelters for day users, fascinating natural and human histories, and a caring staff that does its best to keep the hordes of visitors happy.

Description and special features. Living in nearby Portage, I first walked this park as a child. While I've hiked most of the park's major trails over the years, I rely on the park's informative *Visitor* newspaper for much of the following up-to-date descriptions, the degree of difficulty for each trail, and the approximate time required to hike each.

East Bluff Trails

Balanced Rock. A difficult, steep trail with stone steps on the south face of East Bluff. It has spectacular views, with the quartzite formation of Balanced Rock along the way, is 0.3-mile long, and takes about one hour to hike.

CCC Trail. 👟 👟 👟 👟 👟 A difficult, steep trail with stone steps on the south face of East Bluff. It offers many scenic views in its 0.6-mile length. Approximate hiking time is one hour.

Devil's Doorway. 👟 👟 An easy, level asphalt-paved trail along the edge of the top of the East Bluff features excellent views of Devil's Lake. There is a side trail to Devil's Doorway, a rock formation. The trail is 0.5-mile long and takes approximately fifteen minutes to hike.

East Bluff (orange). 👟 👟 👟 👟 A trail of medium difficulty, asphalt-paved with stone steps, winds between the bluff edge and adjacent woods and has scenic views and drop-offs. Elephant Cave and Elephant Rock are at the north end. Length is 1.3 miles; hiking time is about one hour and fifteen minutes.

East Bluff Woods (yellow). 👟 👟 👟 👟 An easy-to medium-difficulty, gravel and grassy trail through the woods, with a steep grade up the East Bluff from north to south. Length is 1.3 miles; hiking time is about one hour and fifteen minutes.

Grottoes. 👟 👟 An easy, wide, bare earthen path along the bottom of the south end of the East Bluff connecting the Balanced Rock, Potholes, and CCC trails. The 0.7-mile trail takes about half an hour to walk.

Group Camp. 👟 👟 An easy trail that parallels South Shore Road between the Group Camp area and the South Shore picnic area. This 0.4-mile trail takes about half an hour to walk.

Ice Age Loop (red). 👟 👟 👟 👟 A trail of medium difficulty, grassy with variable grades through fields, woods, and brush. There are scenic views from the top of the East Bluff at its south end. This four-mile trail takes about two and one half hours.

Potholes. 👟 👟 👟 👟 👟 A steep trail with stone steps on the south face of the East Bluff. It has scenic views and a series of rounded depressions called potholes near the top. Though it's only 0.3 mile-long, it takes about two hours to climb.

West Bluff Trails

Tumbled Rocks. An easy trail, level and paved, winds through quartzite boulders at the base of the West Bluff just above the lake. Its 0.8 mile takes about half an hour. Heavy rains in 1993 have temporarily closed this trail.

West Bluff (red). A trail of medium difficulty, asphalt paved with stone steps, it climbs steeply on the south end. On the north end, the climb is not as steep, but still difficult. The trail follows the top of the bluff, with scenic views and drop-offs. This 1.5-mile trail takes about 1.5 hours.

Other Trails

Johnson Moraine Loop (white). An easy trail with variable grades crosses County DL twice. It follows the terminal moraine of the Laurentide Ice Sheet on the north side of DL near a number of kettle ponds and marshes. Length is 2.5 miles, taking about two hours to walk.

Steinke Basin Loop (green). An easy trail, grassy and fairly level, goes through an extinct glacial lakebed. There are several bridges and a variety of land cover. Its 2.5 miles takes about two hours.

Ice Age Parfrey's Glen Trail. A new trail goes from the Ice Age Loop Trail near State Highway 113 to Parfrey's Glen, about four miles away. It goes to the bluff-top over boulder-scattered clearings and woods, and then it descends some 750 feet through heavy second-growth woods to the Parfrey's Glen parking lot. Designed as a back-country footpath, according to Gary Werner of the Ice Age Trail and Park Foundation, Inc., it is narrower than most trails in the park proper. The path down the bluff is moderately sloped. The views from the higher segments are worth the trek. (This trail will be closed until summer 1994 because of damage caused by a flash flood in Parfrey's Glen in 1993, says Devil's Lake Park management.)

Self-Guided Walks

Stop by park headquarters for a folder that provides details about the stops on each walk.

Indian Mounds Nature Tour. A walking tour on the north shore grounds takes you to effigy, conical and linear mounds built by the Woodland Culture Indians 1,000 or more years ago.

Landmark Nature Trail. On this south shore tour you can see an Indian mound, the former site of a hotel that existed when Devil's Lake was a private resort area, several tree varieties, and geological formations.

How to get there. The park's headquarters is on the north shore of Devil's Lake. From U.S. 12 2 miles south of Baraboo, go east on State Highway 159 for about 1.5 miles, then south on State Highway 123 for 0.5 mile to the main gate. From State Highway 113 3 miles south of Baraboo, go west on County DL for about 2 miles to the main gate.

When open. Open daily from 6 A.M. to 11 P.M. except for campers coming to their campsites later.

Facilities. Parking, camping (call 608-356-6618 for information), complete picnic facilities including shelters and grills, pit and year-round toilets, swimming beach (swimmer's itch is a common problem for lake swimmers in June and early July), bathhouses, showers (north shore only), boat ramp (no gasoline motors allowed), and three limited-stock retail stores. A state park sticker is required.

Other points of interest in area

Sauk County Historical Museum, 531 Fourth Avenue, Baraboo, has historical artifacts in a three-story mansion. Open mid-May to mid-September, 2 P.M. to 5 P.M. Tuesday through Sunday.

Oschner Park and Zoo, 124 Second Street, Baraboo, has an unusually well stocked zoo for a small city. Open daily.

Circus World Museum, 426 Water Street, Baraboo, is in the former winter quarters of the famous Ringling Brothers Circus. See shows under the big top, demonstrations, concerts, and exhibits. Open 9 A.M. to 6 P.M. daily May to mid-September. A new year-round exhibit also is now open. Telephone 608-356-0800.

For other points of interest see Baraboo Historic Tour, pp. 147–49.

12.4 See Relic, Preserved Plant Types along This Trail

Hemlock Draw, Leland

A number of cuts, hollows, and gorges penetrate the ancient rock of the Baraboo Hills. One of the most fascinating is Hemlock Draw, named for the rare stand of virgin hemlock within its walls.

Description and special features. A 533-acre preserve of the Wisconsin chapter of The Nature Conservancy, this quiet place supports a wide variety of northern and southern Wisconsin trees and shrubs, including dense stands of hemlock, which give the preserve its name. Up to 11 distinct types of vegetative community exist here, according to the Conservancy. Because the site was spared the onslaught of the continental glacier, the edge of which was several miles to the north and east, many relic plant types grow here. The Conservancy protects the rare *Carex prasina*, a sedge, and others. Some 60 species of birds have been sighted. The site is also noted for a pillar of quartzite called a *seastack*.

Degree of difficulty. The trail is primitive with unimproved stream crossings. I found it to be difficult to follow toward its end, but it's well worth the visit. Stay on the trail to avoid destroying rare flora, and take a compass to avoid getting lost.

How to get there. From U.S. 12 midway between Sauk City and Baraboo, go west on County C for about 8 miles to the village of Leland, then north on Hemlock Road to reach Reich Drive, a dead-end graveled lane that goes straight ahead where Hemlock Road veers left. The preserve entrance is about 0.5 mile up Reich Drive, on the right.

When open. The year around, but may be impassable in winter.

Facilities. None.

Other points of interest in area

Natural Bridge State Park is nearby on County C. See pp. 171–73.

5 Trail Leads into Enchanting Birders' Haunt

Honey Creek Preserve

👢 👢 👢

Description and special features. This primitive trail follows the north branch of Honey Creek into a valley it has cut into the Baraboo Hills. So many species of bird have been sighted, including what is believed to be the area's only great blue heron rookery, that the Wisconsin Society for Ornithology (WSO) selected the valley as a site for a preserve in the 1950s. The trail goes through hardwood forests and across old pastureland, mostly between the creek and the sandstone west wall of the valley. It also crosses the creek several times via unimproved crossings.

Ornithologists began buying land for the preserve in the 1950s and now own more than 300 acres. Less than a mile long in the preserve and protected by the walls of the valley, the trail has an air of secluded enchantment usually found only in much more remote locations.

Degree of difficulty. Mostly level but unpaved and often narrow. High water in 1993 made stream crossings more difficult. Wear hiking boots.

How to get there. About 2 miles northwest of Leland on PF, go west on Sky View Road about 0.5 mile. The trailhead, marked by a WSO sign, is on the right.

When open. The year around, but may be impassable in winter.

Facilities. None at the trail. There are pit toilets at the nature center mentioned below.

Other points of interest in area

Across Sky View Road about 80 yards east of the trailhead and south on Alder Drive the society operates Cox Nature Center. Its collection is open to public viewing intermittently.

"Knock on the door" to see if it's open, says society officer Alex Kailing.

Nearby are Natural Bridge State Park, pp. 171–73; Hemlock Draw, pp. 158–59; and White Mound County Park, pp. 174–76.

6 Walk Back in Time Millions of Years

Parfrey's Glen

🥾 🥾 🥾 🥾

The short walk into Parfrey's Glen is figuratively a trip back through millions of years of geologic history. As you gradually ascend into this enchanted place, its ancient geology reveals itself in the towering, stratified sides of the gorge. Because cool air settles to the bottom of the protected glen and its high walls block much of the sunlight, plants and some birds in the upper gorge are more typical of those found hundreds of miles north.

Note: A flash flood in July 1993 forced the closing of the glen. Repair of damage will be completed and the glen reopened "sometime in 1994," according to a park spokesperson.

Description. From the parking lot just north of County DL walk a blacktop former road that curves up to the glen for about one-third mile. The road ends at an old parking lot not used since auto travel this far was banned.

The path slowly ascends into the glen and culminates in a man-made stone terrace with a serene view of a small waterfall and rapids cascading out of the Baraboo Bluffs. Return by same route.

Since Parfrey's Glen is a protected scientific area, walkers are required to stay on the path to avoid trampling rare plants or defacing geologic formations. Regulations prohibit picnicking, pets, and camping.

Special features. From the parking lot to the end of the old asphalt road the path takes you on a wide curve through a grassy meadow. In the spring look for an array of wildflowers: Dutchman's breeches, swamp buttercup, and pasqueflower, among others. In summer I also saw yellow goatsbeard near the parking lot. Cottonwood, oaks, and a few maples are scattered on the grassland.

As you walk into the glen, the environment transforms into that of a hardwood forest. About 300 yards into the glen, look on the left for several colonies of a short spearlike plant segmented like bamboo. This is called scouring rush. Because of its high silica content, early settlers used the plant to scour pots and pans.

On the left another 40 yards or so up the trail is the old, barely discernible foundation of a gristmill that was operated by Robert Parfrey, owner of the glen, shortly after the Civil War. The story is told that a pre–Civil War distillery in the glen converted rye from nearby fields into a potent "mountain dew" with the aid of the flowing creek.

Walking up the path you'll become increasingly aware of the gentle strumming of the creek as background music to nature's proud display. Starting at about 360 yards into the glen with the first stream crossing, the difficulty of the path increases progressively. Stop here if you're not sure-footed. With this crossing and others, test the stepping stones first for slipperiness, and make sure your hands are free to catch yourself if you slip.

At about 425 yards the stratified walls of the gorge give clues to the geologic history of the area. The bottom-most layer of Cambrian rock is between 500 million and 600 million years old. Higher layers are progressively younger. Notice the intermittent layers of broken and water-worn stones. These quartzite fragments were cemented into sandstone representing ancient beaches from a time when water covered the area. After two more tricky stream crossings, you'll notice more layered walls on the right.

Because cool air settles to the bottom of the gorge and sunlight is largely blocked out, flora in the upper gorge is more typical of that found in northern Wisconsin. Look for yellow birch and mountain maple, as well as the winter wren and Canada warbler.

About 475 yards into the gorge a boardwalk takes you over an area that is sometimes wet. On the left notice the delicate ferns and other plants that thrive in this cool, dim environment.

Perhaps 50 yards further you'll notice giant boulders of sandstone with water-washed quartzite pebbles and cobbles embedded in them. These conglomerate boulders are called plum pudding—the sandstone is the pudding in which the quartzite stones are suspended. Slab rock stairs in the trail take you up among the boulders.

Just past the boulders the trail ends with a delightful surprise—an unexpected overlook of a waterfall where the stream cascades out of the bluffs.

While bedrock in the bottom of the gorge may be as old as 600 million years, geologists believe the gorge itself was formed only about 12,000 years ago. When the last continental glacier receded, meltwater formed a violently rushing river much larger than the present-day stream. It quickly eroded this cut into the shallower valley that once existed there.

Degree of difficulty. A wide and easy walkway at first, the trail becomes narrower and steeper with some stairs as it ascends deeper into the gorge. You must cross Parfrey's Glen stream several times using midstream rocks as stepping stones. Distance into the glen is less than a mile.

How to get there. From I-90–94 several miles south of Portage, go west on State Highway 78 for 8 miles, then right on County DL, just west of the Sauk County border, for 2 miles. The entrance, on the right, is marked by a small sign that's easy to miss.

Approaching from the west from State Highway 113 about halfway between Baraboo and Merrimac, go east on County DL for 2 miles to the entrance on the left.

Facilities. Parking, pit toilets, drinking water.

Other points of interest in area

Devil's Lake State Park. Turn right from Parfrey's Glen parking lot and follow DL for 2 miles, turn right onto State Highway 113, and take the next road left into the park. There are trails for the seasoned hiker and the casual stroller. Open the year around. (See pp. 153–57 for information about trails.)

A new Parfrey's Glen segment of the Ice Age Trail goes west from the Glen's parking lot to the Ice Age Loop Trail in Devil's Lake State Park. It's also described in the chapter mentioned above about the state park. Because of the above-mentioned flash flood this trail will be closed until Parfrey's Glen is reopened.

Devil's Head Resort. Turn left from Parfrey's Glen parking lot and go 0.2 mile on DL, then turn left onto Bluff Road and go 0.4

mile to the driveway on the right. This private resort offers skiing in the winter and golf during other seasons. It has 13 ski lifts and 20 runs from bunny to expert, an 18-hole golf course, two restaurants, a lodge, and condos (telephone 608 493-2251 or 1-800-DEVILSX).

Colsac Ferry. Turning left from the Parfrey's Glen parking lot, take County DL for 0.2 mile, then turn right onto Bluff Road and go about 3.5 miles to Merrimac. One of the few remaining public car ferries in Wisconsin crosses Lake Wisconsin at Merrimac from April to November. The twelve-car ferry is free and takes about eight minutes to cross, but you may wait a lot longer during times of heavy traffic, especially in summer. The name *Colsac* is derived from the two counties the ferry serves, Columbia on the south landing and Sauk on the north.

7 Take a Hike Where Eagles Roost

Ferry Bluff Eagle Sanctuary

"How can I soar with eagles when I spend my days working with turkeys?" one wag lamented. Well, here's an opportunity at least to hike where eagles roost and soar. It's on a bluff high over the Wisconsin River in southern Sauk County. The National Wildlife Federation funded the purchase of this sanctuary, which is protected as a State of Wisconsin Natural Area.

Description and special features. This trail starts where Honey Creek flows into the Wisconsin River. It follows the river west for several hundred yards before ascending Cactus Bluff, the center of three side-by-side bluffs. Not only eagles inhabit this preserve. Watch for the swallows, redwing blackbirds, warblers, and pairs of mallards that are attracted to the river.

Completed in 1992, a new path up the bluff crisscrosses it to make the grade less steep. When you reach the top, you'll be treated to a panoramic view of the river and valley.

Degree of difficulty. Easy-to-walk natural turf along the river, becoming steeper but well constructed on the bluff with woodchip surface.

How to get there. From its junction with U.S. 12 just north of Sauk City, go west on State Highway 60 for 4.2 miles to Ferry Bluff Road, on the left. This dirt road may be hard to find. It was not marked when I visited the bluff. Going west on 60, if you reach County B go back—you've gone too far. Take Ferry Bluff Road south 1 mile to the river. Park along the road.

When open. April 1 to November 14. It's closed the rest of the year to avoid disturbing the eagles' roost, according to Dave Gjestson, DNR Lower Wisconsin Riverway coordinator.

Facilities. There is a drop-off point for passengers of motored vehicles at trailhead. You can park along the road near the drop-off point.

8 Retreat from Busy Tourists' Mecca to Quiet Wooded Trails

Mirror Lake State Park, Lake Delton

👟 👟

Located just a mile from the edge of the blatantly commercialized "amusement park" that is the Wisconsin Dells–Lake Delton area, Mirror Lake Park trails offer a quiet reprieve.

Description and special features. Construction of a dam across Dell Creek formed Mirror Lake in a picturesque sandstone gorge. As is also true of the Dells of the Wisconsin River several miles to the north, the gorge was formed some 10,000 years ago by the rushing waters released from Glacial Lake Wisconsin. Formed by a glacial ice dam, the large lake in what is now central Wisconsin drained suddenly as the continental glacier retreated.

The torrent wore into the plain exposing late Cambrian sandstone laid down 500 million years ago. Though the glacier never quite reached this area, its meltwater etched ripples and ruts into the sides of the gorge in beautiful patterns viewed by canoeists and hikers today.

The trails in this 2,000-acre park wind through hardwood forests and along bluffs, spiked with tall white pine, that surround the lake. Two self-guiding informational trails, the Time Warp Trail and the Nature Trail, warrant your special attention. Before walking them, stop at the park office to obtain an informational booklet for each one.

Time Warp Trail. This 0.4-mile trail lets you explore the past, present, and future of one of the most diverse pieces of terrain in the park, the area around Blue Water Bay. Informational stops explain how changes in the lake and the surrounding land have affected the types and condition of plants and animals that inhabit the area.

Nature Trail. Informational stops along this 0.7-mile trail identify trees and shrubs found in the sandy soils throughout the park.

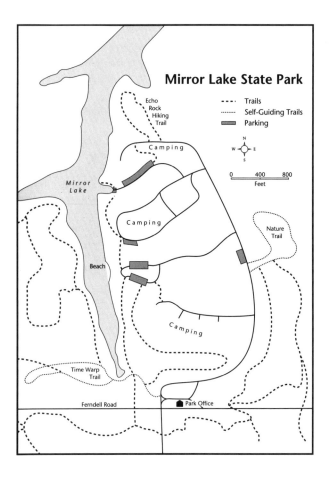

Mirror Lake State Park

- - - Trails
.... Self-Guiding Trails
▬ Parking

Echo
Rock
Hiking
Trail

Camping

Mirror
Lake

Camping

Nature
Trail

Beach

Camping

Time Warp
Trail

Ferndell Road   Park Office

0   400   800
Feet

Degree of difficulty. A selection of looping trails vary from less than 1 mile to 2.7 miles in length and total about 18 miles. The park is hilly, but trails are wide and well-maintained natural turf.

How to get there. From U.S. 12 near I-90-94 take exit 92 (Baraboo–Wisconsin Dells), go west on Ferndell Road for about 1.2 miles to the park entrance on the right.

When open. You may walk these trails any day of the year. The park office is open from 8 A.M. to 11 P.M. daily June through August and 8 A.M. to 4:30 P.M. other months. A state park sticker is required.

Facilities. Camping with electrical hookups and showers, picnicking areas, pit toilets, swimming beach. Snowmobiling and cross-country skiing are allowed.

Other points of interest in area

No visit to the Wisconsin Dells area is complete without experiencing the original attraction upon which the tourist business was built, the Upper and Lower Dells boat rides. You can see the famous Wisconsin River dells from the comfort of a double-decker tour boat or from a World War II amphibian "duck." Ticket booths in strategic places throughout the Wisconsin Dells area provide information about schedules and prices (about $15 for the ducks to under $10 for the tour boats). Boats run from April through October.

On a guided tour at the International Crane Foundation you'll see some of the most beautiful and rare birds on earth. While the main purpose of the foundation is to increase crane populations and reintroduce them into their natural habitats throughout the world, a visit to this place also provides valuable insights on how to preserve and protect them in the wild. Take U.S. 12 north from Baraboo or south from Lake Delton, then turn east on Shady Lane at the foundation's sign. Open daily from Memorial Day through Labor Day and on weekends in September and October. Prices: $3.75 for adults, $1.75 for children ages 5–11, free under age 5.

In its 50 acres of circus life in Baraboo, the city where the

Ringling Bros. Circus originated, the Circus World Museum has circus acts, exhibits of parade wagons, musical instruments, a side show, and a carousel. Open from early May through mid September. Prices: under $10 for adults, under $6 for children 3–12, toddlers free.

9 Native Americans Lived beneath This Bridge 500 Generations Ago

Natural Bridge State Park, Leland

🥾 🥾 🥾

Follow a trail to a wind-carved stone bridge and rock shelter that is one of the oldest sites of human occupation in the Midwest. Paleo-Indians and their descendants lived on this site starting 10,000 to 12,000 years ago, according to radio-carbon dating of remains of habitation found there.

Description and special features. The park has two adjoining trails. You can reach the *Indian Moccasin Nature Trail,* which is about half a mile long, from a spur going north from the parking lot. The longer Whitetail Hiking Trail is connected to the former trail. You can also reach it by going west from the parking lot.

The focus of the Indian Moccasin Trail, of course, is the natural bridge and rock shelter. You can reach it fastest by going left from the end of the parking lot spur.

Formed from wind erosion of sandstone, assisted by rain, frost, and gravity, the bridge has an opening that is about 25 feet high and 35 feet wide. The largest natural bridge in Wisconsin, it has attracted area residents for picnics, Independence Day celebrations, and just plain sightseeing since the 1870s and possibly earlier.

Archaeologists have recognized the rock shelter beneath the bridge as an ancient site of human occupation for years. The June 1959 issue of *The Wisconsin Archaeologist* carried three articles about the archaeology and geology of the site.

Further along the trail you'll climb to a scenic overlook looking northwest into the western Baraboo hills. Descend from the overlook via stairs, and the trail loops back to the spur.

Twenty-eight informational stops along the Moccasin Trail identify trees and shrubs and tell of their early uses as medicines and for other purposes by Native Americans.

Be prepared for a steep climb up the *Whitetail Trail.* Autumn is the best time of year to climb this ridge. In this mature southern Wisconsin oak forest, old oaks have given way to the

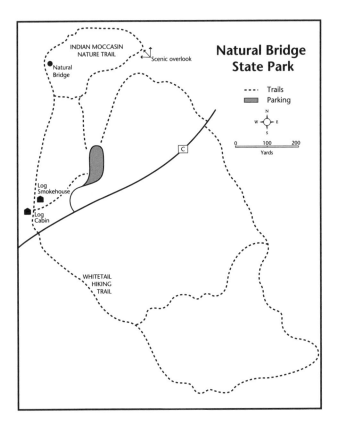

**Natural Bridge
State Park**

INDIAN MOCCASIN
NATURE TRAIL

Natural
Bridge

Scenic overlook

Log
Smokehouse

Log
Cabin

WHITETAIL
HIKING
TRAIL

C

Trails
Parking

N
W   E
S

0   100   200
Yards

bright yellows and reds of maples, aspens, and basswoods, forming an umbrella overhead and carpet beneath of bright reds and yellows.

Degree of difficulty. Both the Indian Moccasin Trail, on which the natural bridge is located, and the Whitetail Trail, which ascends and follows a ridge on the east side of County C, slope steeply. The Moccasin Trail is wide and largely well maintained. The less frequently used Whitetail Trail becomes narrow as it follows the ridge. Total distance for all trails is about 3.5 miles.

How to get there. From U.S. 12 midway between Baraboo and Sauk City, go west on County C for 10 miles to the park entrance on left.

When open. The year around from dawn to dusk. A state park naturalist assists visitors on weekends during the summer. Although a state park admission sticker is required, enforcement is infrequent.

Facilities. Included in the 530-acre park are an old log home and smokehouse, a parking lot, pit toilets, and a picnic area. There are no overnight camping facilities.

Other points of interest in area

Hemlock Draw, a preserve of The Nature Conservancy, is a quiet place that supports a wide variety of northern and southern Wisconsin vegetation within its sandstone walls, as well as some 60 species of birds. (See pp. 158–59.)

Baxter's Hollow is The Nature Conservancy's largest preserve in the Baraboo Hills. (See pp. 150–51.)

10 Walk a Nature Trail and See an Old Lime Kiln

White Mound County Park

Conservationists dammed Honey Creek in 1969 to control flooding and formed the 110-acre White Mound Lake. The 1,100-acre park surrounding the lake soon followed.

One of the charms of this diversified recreation facility is that relatively few users have discovered it. While regularly cleared, trails are so infrequently used that occasional wildflowers grow right on them. Walkers can enjoy the solitude usually reserved for much more remotely located trails.

Description and special features. The park has three walking or hiking trails. The lakeside trail generally follows the margins of the lake. The kiln trail branches off of the lakeside trail from near the south shore. The nature trail is reached from a spur going to the beach and from other access points.

The lake is stocked with bass, bluegills, northern and wall-eyed pike, and catfish to provide year-round fishing. Due to agricultural runoff into Honey Creek, the water is not the clearest, but a beach offers swimming and sunbathing.

Walking trails are:

Lakeside Trail. The longest of the three trails, it traverses both woodland and open prairie. You'll experience excellent views of the lake from many points. A variety of wildflowers border the trail in spring and summer. Several signs along the way highlight such features as a hillside food patch provided for wildlife.

Nature Trail. The gem of White Mound Park, this half-mile trail provides an outdoor class in woodland ecology. Before walking this trail, be sure to stop at the park office for a copy of the nature trail guide, which describes and explains the 26 marked stops along the way. Written by two University of Wisconsin ecologists in cooperation with park supervisor Harland

Schneider, the guide sheds light on the many easily missed signs of plant and animal activity.

Kiln Trail. leads to a restored stone lime kiln believed to be built in the mid-nineteenth century. A sign at the kiln tells how it was used.

Degree of difficulty. The trail around the lake is wide and easy, but watch for the few unexpected ruts and holes. The kiln trail is strenuous, involving many steps and a fairly steep climb. The nature trail is moderately easy, with some small upgrades and ravines. Maintenance of trails is good. The three trails total about five miles in length.

How to get there. From State Highway 23 about 13 miles north of Spring Green, go west on County GG for a fraction of a mile to Lake Road, on the right, which takes you to White Mound County Park entrance.

Facilities. The park is fully developed. In addition to hiking trails, it offers snowmobiling, cross-country skiing, and equestrian trails. You can reserve a low-cost campsite with or without electrical service by calling 608-546-5011. The park has two large picnic shelters, grills, play areas, boat launch, and plenty of toilet facilities.

Other points of interest in area

The focal point of Natural Bridge State Park, a 530-acre dayuse park that offers hiking, snowmobiling, and picnicking, is a natural sandstone arch. Take County C northeast a few miles from Leland. State park daily or annual fee. (See pp. 171–73.)

Our Lady of the Fields Shrine, an enchanting little chapel built by area pioneers, is located a few miles west of White Mound Park. From Lake Road take County GG west to Loreto, then County G north to Chapel Road. No charge.

Wisconsin Society for Ornithology Honey Creek Preserve is little-known, short, and easy and follows a stream where bird watching is excellent. Due east of White Mound Park and west of Natural Bridge Park take Skyview Road a fraction of a mile west from County PF. Trail is to the right, marked by "WSO" sign. (See pp. 160–61.)

Western Baraboo Bluffs. Bright autumn yellows, reds, and oranges of the many maples will dazzle you when you drive from Leland to North Freedom on County PF. Peak colors vary annually from about October 1 to October 20. You can buy newly picked apples and fresh cider at Maple Hill Orchard along the way.

Walworth County

April 1, 1851.—What a lovely walk! Clear sky, rising sun, all the tints vivid, all the contours distinct, save the softly misty and infinite lake . . . and all the countryside a tone of vigorous health, youth and freshness.

THE PRIVATE JOURNAL OF HENRI-FRÉDÉRIC AMIEL

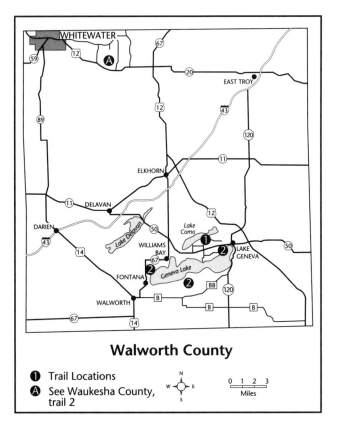

Walworth County

● Trail Locations
Ⓐ See Waukesha County, trail 2

N
W — E
S

0 1 2 3
Miles

1 Escape the Busy Tourist Scene along an Old Railroad Bed

Duck Lake Nature Trail, Lake Geneva

👟 👟

A quiet three-mile trail follows a railroad bed along the lowlands bordering the southeast shore of Lake Como (formerly called Duck Lake).

Description and special features. Following the gently curving path of the abandoned Chicago & Northwestern Railroad bed through woods and lakeside bottomlands, this trail has solitude as its chief virtue. Few people outside the local area know about it so it provides an opportunity to temporarily escape the helter-skelter tourist scene of the Lake Geneva area.

While numbered posts on the trail identify flora described in a separate printed nature guide, some posts are missing and the guide is not readily available anymore, but this doesn't detract from the trail itself. The charm of this place is its quietness.

Degree of difficulty. Level and grassy, the trail is easy to walk. Several wood bridges were in poor repair but were passable when I walked the trail. A branch of the trail, the "Ernest Roeker Trail," descends into the lakeside bottomland. Since it seemed not well marked and hard to follow, I did not take it far.

How to get there. To enter from the west end, take Schofield Road north from State Highway 50 about 1.5 miles west of the Lake Geneva city limits. Near Lake Como, at the intersection of Schofield and South Shore Drive, park and walk east on a private road to the trailhead.

There is also an entrance from Grand View Drive just west of Lake Geneva.

When open. The year around. The trail is not cleared of snow in winter.

Facilities. There are several benches along the trail.

Other points of interest in area

See Geneva Lake Shoreline Path, pp. 181–85.

2 Chicago's Wealthiest Families Lived in Mansions on This Path

Geneva Lake Shoreline Path

The 26-mile path around Geneva Lake is unique for several reasons. One is that it still exists at all. Following the beaches, bays, and points of the lake's irregular shore, it crosses hundreds of privately and publicly owned properties. While private landowners have in the past opposed hikers crossing their land, the courts have declared that since the path existed as a publicly used trail before the property was privately held, the public's right to continue traveling it is preserved.

And oh, those landowners! Descending on the area from Chicago in the late 1800s after the Great Chicago Fire, they bought large tracts and built mansions the likes of which Wisconsin had rarely seen. Tax rolls during that time must have read like a Who's Who of Chicago millionaires—the Wrigleys, the Swifts, the Bordens, the Drakes, the Wackers, to name a few.

If you tire of reviewing the parade of mansions on one side as you walk, rest your eyes on one of the state's clearest large lakes on the other.

Description and special features. Starting from the small Flatiron Park in Lake Geneva and going clockwise around the lake, you will pass these mansions:

Stone Manor is one of the most impressive of a group of mansions near the city. The Italianate structure is 175 feet long with a 250-foot veranda. Builder Otto Young, a Chicago industrialist, had images of his four daughters sculpted into the exterior. A developer recently converted the 50,000-square-foot mansion into seven elegant condominiums.

Just past this group of mansions, Big Foot Beach State Park occupies 272 acres, including 1,900 feet of shoreline of which about 900 is sandy beach. Much of the acreage was once owned by the son of Fred Maytag of the washing machine company. Maytag built a lagoon in the shape of Geneva Lake, which now is a centerpiece of the park's picnic grounds.

Several miles down the shoreline, past a restaurant that was

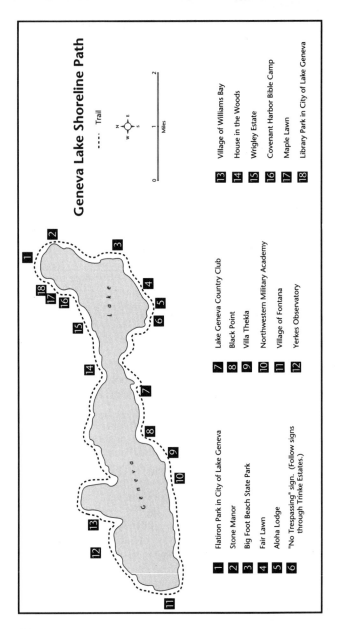

Geneva Lake Shoreline Path

0   1   2
Miles

---- Trail

1   Flatiron Park in City of Lake Geneva
2   Stone Manor
3   Big Foot Beach State Park
4   Fair Lawn
5   Aloha Lodge
6   "No Trespassing" sign. (Follow signs through Trinke Estates.)

7   Lake Geneva Country Club
8   Black Point
9   Villa Thekla
10   Northwestern Military Academy
11   Village of Fontana
12   Yerkes Observatory

13   Village of Williams Bay
14   House in the Woods
15   Wrigley Estate
16   Covenant Harbor Bible Camp
17   Maple Lawn
18   Library Park in City of Lake Geneva

once the mansion of J. H. Dow of Dow-Jones fame, Fair Lawn was built in 1884 by Charles H. Wacker, citizen of Chicago after whom Wacker Drive was named.

West of Fair Lawn, Tracey Drake of Drake Hotels built an estate he called Aloha Lodge. You'll trek through some lowlands and run into a No Trespassing sign at Hillside Road bordering Trinke Estates. To get through this area, follow Hillside Road south from the lake to Burr Oak Drive, go right and follow the signs. Next is Lake Geneva Country Club, said to be the oldest private golf links in the Midwest.

Several miles west, Chicago industrialist Conrad Siepp built a mansion at Black Point. From a four-story tower the Siepps, who still own the estate, get a commanding view of the lake. Another notable mansion, just west of Black Point, Villa Thekla, was built on a high hill overlooking the lake.

Between Black Point and Fontana, Northwestern Military Academy is a college preparatory school built in 1915. Scenes in the motion picture *Damien-Omen II* were filmed here in 1976.

At the west end of the lake you'll reach Fontana, a pleasant village whose major industry appears to be the mooring of yachts and some smaller craft. There are also three golf courses in the village. Around the end of the lake northeast of Fontana, on a hill above Williams Bay, Yerkes Observatory, owned by the University of Chicago, has the world's largest refracting telescope. Tours are conducted on Saturdays.

A sometimes rocky, sloped path east of Williams Bay will take you to the House in the Woods, one of the more impressive estates with a reflecting pool and a U-shaped house with 78-foot wings. The estate occupies 44 acres. Not far to the east, the Wrigleys of the chewing gum business and past owners of the Chicago Cubs baseball team own a Georgian-style brick home. About a mile to the east, the Covenant Harbor Bible Camp was once the estate of the Borden family.

The first large mansion built on the lake, Maple Lawn, is several blocks east in the city of Lake Geneva. Go farther east to reach Library Park, on which the city's library is located. The park also has a large expanse of public beach.

Degree of difficulty. Since each property owner decides the type of paving on his or her portion of the trail, surfaces vary widely—from a concrete walk across some properties to little visible trail at all across others. Maintenance also varies from good to none.

Both pavement and maintenance tend to be best in or near the municipalities the trail goes through. During my springtime walk I sampled both rural and in-town portions. The trail was often blocked by stacks of pier members, especially in rural areas. Several residents assured me, however, that this was not the case in summer.

It was difficult to see exactly where the trail went in some little-used areas. As mentioned above, a fence and No Trespassing sign blocked at least one portion of the south shore, at Trinke Estates, and only after searching did I find that the trail resumed farther south on Hillside Road.

The shoreline elevation the path follows varies from lake-level beaches to steep, though not very high, cliffs. Aside from its 26-mile length, the walk is not especially strenuous.

How to get there. Geneva Lake is in southern Walworth County. You may enter the trail from any public park or access point. I suggest starting from any of the three towns on the trail, Lake Geneva, Fontana, or Williams Bay, where parking is available.

When open. Spring, summer, and fall. Many portions are impassable when there is appreciable snow cover.

Facilities. Public parks in towns along the trail have varying facilities, including toilets and picnic grounds. Each town has a variety of restaurants.

Other points of interest in area

Big Foot Beach State Park on the east shore of the lake has 100 campsites that are available from May through October. For information about reservations call 414-248-2528. There are 31 acres of picnic and play area, a 900-foot beach with two bathhouses, and an eight-acre lagoon. More than four miles of trails include 0.7-mile self-guided nature trail. A state park sticker is required.

Geneva Lake Cruise Line offers sightseeing, luncheon and

dinner cruises on the lake from May 1 through October 31. Boats leave from the pier in Lake Geneva. For a schedule call 1-800-558-5911. A fee is charged.

You may tour Yerkes Observatory at 1:30, 2:15, or 3 P.M. Saturday from June through September, and at 10 A.M. or noon other months. The observatory is on State Highway 67 on the west side of the village of Williams Bay.

The Duck Lake Nature Trail in the Town of Geneva follows an old railroad bed near Lake Como. See pp. 179–80.

Washington County

A book that says anything about walking has a ready passage to my inmost heart.

Christopher Morley, THE ART OF WALKING

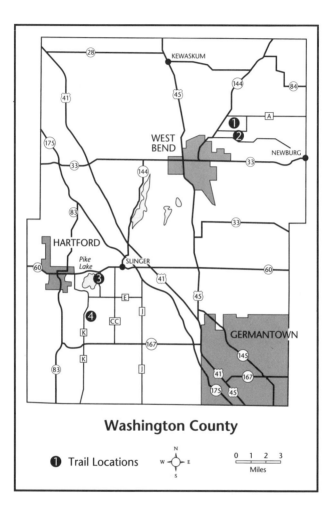

Washington County

1 Trail Locations

N
W · E
S

0 1 2 3
Miles

1 Walk a Trail among Archaeological Treasures

Lizard Mound County Park

👟 👟

We know about ancient Egyptians because they built the pyramids, which remain today. Early Europeans drew pictures in caves depicting the animals they hunted. In Wisconsin and nearby between about A.D. 800 and 1200, the Woodland Culture Indians built earthen mounds in the shapes of animals, birds, hemispheres, ovals, and linear configurations.

You can see 25 of these monuments along a trail in Lizard Mound County Park, which the county acquired from the state in 1986.

Description and special features. The mile-long trail zigzags through the wooded park from one mound to another. Along the way are examples of panthers, birds, a bear, conical and linear mounds, and, of course, the lizard mound after which the park was named. Most are in an excellent state of preservation.

Two sets of informational stations provide the walker with facts about this unique place. One tells about the mounds and their builders; the other identifies trees and shrubs.

Degree of difficulty. The path is unpaved but wide and level. During my walk there in November 1993, I noticed that the thick blanket of leaves had been raked from the mounds and the path, to make them more easily visible.

How to get there. From West Bend go northeast on State Highway 144 for several miles, then east 0.3 mile on County A to the park entrance on the right.

When open. From April 1 to November 30. You can walk the trail at other times if you park outside the gate and walk in about one-quarter mile.

Facilities. Parking, picnic tables, grills, drinking water, and pit toilets, which are closed during the off-season.

Other points of interest in area

To the northwest about six miles near Kewaskum starts the Northern Unit of the Kettle Moraine State Forest. There you'll find ten hiking or nature trails among its kettles, kames, eskers, and other glacially deposited landforms. The forest is open the year around for hiking. A state park sticker is required.

2 Park Boasts Four Trails and Activities for the Entire Family

Sandy Knoll County Park, West Bend

Bring the kids when you go to this 267-acre park. You can not only walk its four trails but also swim, fish, picnic, or play softball, volleyball, or even basketball.

Description and special features. Trails wind through a variety of environments. Three of them form a triple set of loops through a new stand of hardwoods with some old birches sprinkled in, over a prairie, and around wetlands. Bright white posts with colored stripes mark each trail.

Degree of difficulty. The soft, sandy natural surface of these trails makes them easy on the feet. The terrain is gently undulating. The black trail, looping around soggy lowlands, has a reputation for being mosquito infested during the summer. Park management carefully maintains trails and the entire park.

How to get there. From State Highway 144 just northeast of West Bend go east on Wallace Lake Road for 1.5 miles. You'll find the park entrance on the left just east of North Trenton Road.

When open. The year around from 7 A.M. to 9 P.M.

Facilities. A small pond with a swimming beach, but no dressing rooms, is stocked for trout fishing. The park also has facilities for softball, volleyball, basketball, horseshoes, and picnicking, including several enclosed shelters. Drinking water and year-around toilets are available. You may cross-country ski on three of the four hiking trails. There are five parking lots.

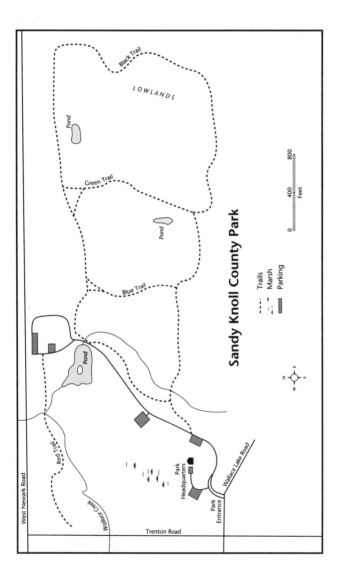

Sandy Knoll County Park

Trails
Marsh
Parking

Black Trail

LOWLANDS

Pond

Green Trail

Pond

Blue Trail

Pond

Red Trail

West Newark Road

Wallace Creek

Wallace Lake Road

Park Headquarters

Park Entrance

Trenton Road

N
W E
S

0   400   800
Feet

Other points of interest in area

West Bend and nearby Jackson are bargain hunters' magnets. Shoppers frequent the factory stores of Amity Leather, on State Highway 33 east in West Bend, and Bieri Cheese, in Jackson, as well as the large West Bend Factory Outlet Mall, 180 Island Avenue.

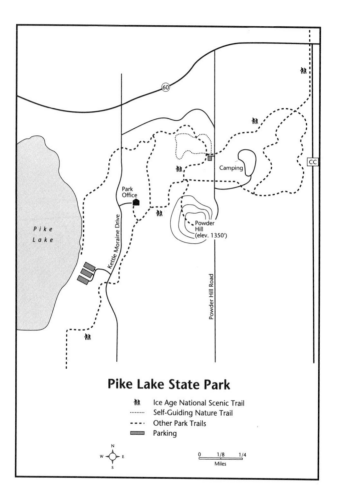

Pike Lake State Park

🚶 Ice Age National Scenic Trail
.... Self-Guiding Nature Trail
- - - - Other Park Trails
▭ Parking

N
W ✦ E
S

0   1/8   1/4
Miles

3 Pick Your Season To Climb a Kame

Pike Lake State Park, Hartford

If you had an opportunity to walk a kettle moraine trail through a hardwood forest of towering oaks and hickories with a few maples, beeches, and basswoods thrown in you'd probably go in autumn, when the colors are most brilliant. If you also could climb a giant conical hill to get a hawk's-eye view of the hummocky scenery for miles around, you'd most certainly pick a clear day to do it.

Only if you were trying to finish writing a book about walks by a certain date would you take such a walk in Pike Lake State Park near Hartford on a foggy day in March, as I did. But I found that even then a hike over trails covered with the wet snow and spongy ice of late winter to the top of Powder Hill, an unusually high kame, is rewarding. The fog provided a cushion of stillness interrupted only by the faint trickle of meltwater bubbling from under the ice. I hoped the fog would clear by the time I reached the top of the hill so I could enjoy the view, but it didn't. However, I experienced a real sense of accomplishment just by reaching the 1,350-foot crest up the steep, icy trail.

Description and special features. Located between the northern and southern units of the Kettle Moraine State Forest, 678-acre Pike Lake State Park has all the features of glacial sculpturing. Like crumpled ribbons trails loop over eskers and down into kettles. A spur climbs one of the highest kames, an enormous pile of sediment deposited by water seeping through a crack in the glacier as it melted, in Wisconsin.

From the top of the kame on a clear day you can see the First Wisconsin Bank building 25 miles to the southeast in downtown Milwaukee, according to John Wald, park superintendent. The twin spires of the Catholic shrine devoted to St. Mary atop Holy Hill, another giant Kame in Washington County, are visible seven miles to the south.

The park's namesake, 40-foot-deep Pike Lake, was formed in a glacial kettle. Some eight miles of trails in the park include a segment of the Ice Age National Scenic Trail that runs diagonally through the park and connects to a segment leading to Holy Hill. (See pp. 197–99.) There is also a three-quarter-mile nature trail.

Degree of difficulty. Even excluding the path up Powder Hill, trails are often steep and mostly unpaved, but wide and well maintained. Wood chips carpet some of the steepest portions to prevent erosion and reduce slipperiness during wet weather. The climb to the top of Powder Hill includes some broad steps, solidly constructed of railroad ties.

How to get there. From Hartford go east on State Highway 60 for 3 miles, turn south into the park on Kettle Moraine Drive, and go about 0.5 mile to park headquarters on the left.

When open. The year around from 6 A.M. to 11 P.M. except for overnight campers.

Facilities. Camping with 32 sites from May to October (no electricity), picnic tables, and grills as well as a small shelter. A beach on the springfed lake offers swimming with dressing rooms, toilets, and showers. (In winter, the park sets up portable toilets near the beach for ice fishers and other park users.) Although the park has no boat ramp, several public and private ramps are available elsewhere on the lake. You may park at the park headquarters or in the big lakeside lot a little farther south on Kettle Moraine Drive.

Other points of interest in area

Hartford, three miles west of the park, is a city of about 7,000 with an interesting history. At city hall, 109 North Main Street, you can obtain a brochure describing a walking tour of historical sites. One of the tour's highlights, the Hartford Heritage Auto Museum, has a group of Kissel luxury autos of the type that were manufactured in the city from 1906 to 1931.

4 Follow the Green Bay Terminal Moraine to Holy Hill

Holy Hill Segment, Ice Age National Scenic Trail, near Hartford

👟 👟 👟 👟

Going over privately owned land, this portion of the Ice Age National Scenic Trail traces the Green Bay moraine between Pike Lake State Park, near Hartford and Slinger, and Donegal Road, just south of Holy Hill. You'll view a succession of glacial features, including Holy Hill itself, a kame with an elevation of 1,335 feet.

Description and special features. At its north end, the segment connects with the Ice Age National Scenic Trail segment in Pike Lake State Park. Going south from the park you will cross County E and Glassgo Drive. Watch for a prominent kettle on the left between Glassgo and Waterford Road. Not too far past Pleasant Hill Road, look for a tree stump on the left with a yellow arrow drawn on it. The arrow points at a marvelously symmetrical kame some distance to the east.

Farther on, before you reach Shannon Road, you will pass an old sugar maple with a circumference of 11.5 feet. The trail enters Holy Hill property south of State Highway 167 and continues around the side of the giant moulin kame, which was deposited in a mill hole in the ice sheet as meltwaters swirled into it.

Hiking over a succession of landowners' property, you'll go through mixed hardwood and pine forests, much of which is second growth. The trail traverses stone fences of glacial boulders as well as grasslands, some of which apparently had been under the plow in the recent past.

Degree of difficulty. The hummocky terrain, typical of moraines, provides an interesting and varied hike with many slopes and inclines. Though some slopes are steep, they're mostly short and easy to walk. Designed as a back-country footpath, the trail is sometimes narrow and mostly natural turf. It frequently meanders to add to the variety of surrounding

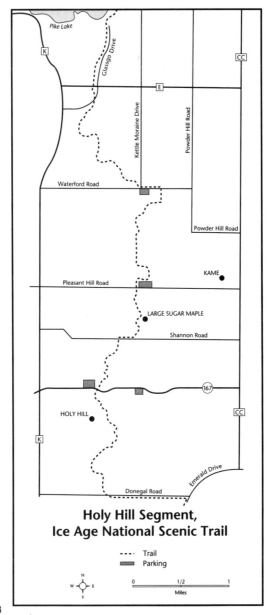

Holy Hill Segment,
Ice Age National Scenic Trail

- - - - Trail
▭ Parking

N
W ⊕ E
S

0   1/2   1
Miles

landforms and vegetation the hiker will experience. Yellow blazes on trees and posts clearly mark the path.

How to get there. A good starting place is the beach area in Pike Lake State Park, just west of Hartford and south of State Highway 60, where parking is ample. You may also enter the trail from Waterford Road, Pleasant Hill Road, or State Highway 167, where there are a few roadside parking spaces. Or park in the lot at the Holy Hill shrine or at the Stations Way Road picnic area, just east of the trail south of Highway 167. There are no parking spaces on Donegal Road at the south end of the trail.

When open. The year around. The trail is not groomed in winter. No camping, picnicking, or fires are allowed on private land. Please stay on the trail.

Facilities. There are rest rooms at the beach area of Pike Lake, with portable toilets provided during the winter. Parking is available as mentioned above.

Other points of interest in area

Holy Hill, 1525 Carmel Road, Hubertus, has a large Romanesque Catholic shrine staffed by the Discalced Carmelite Order of Friars. On the grounds are an outdoor Way of the Cross, the National Shrine Chapel of Mary, a Lourdes Grotto, a Chapel of St. Therese, picnic areas, and a gift store. Holy Hill provides a panorama of the surrounding kettle moraine.

Waukesha County

Man takes root at his feet, and at best he is no more than a potted plant in his house or carriage till he has established communication with the soil by the loving and magnetic touch of his soles to it.

John Burroughs, THE EXHILARATIONS OF THE ROAD

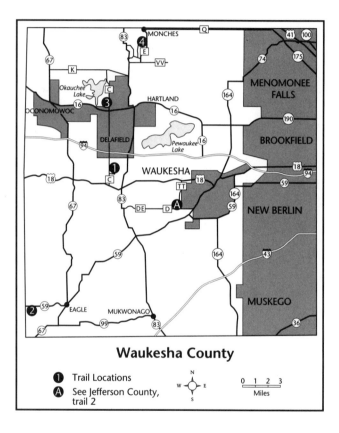

Waukesha County

1 Trail Locations

A See Jefferson County, trail 2

0 1 2 3 Miles

1 Trails Lead to Waukesha County's Highest Point

Lapham Peak Unit, Kettle Moraine State Forest, Delafield

👟 👟 👟 👟

When Increase Lapham, pioneer Wisconsin scientist and founder of the U.S. Weather Service, established a signal station on 1,233-foot-high Government Hill in 1870, his purpose was to be able to warn ports on the Great Lakes of approaching storms. He'd be surprised to learn that this highest hill in Waukesha County was renamed in his honor and became part of a state forest known for its challenging hiking trails.

Description and special features. Four trails loop through the 671-acre forest, and a certified segment of the Ice Age National Scenic Trail goes from the southeast corner to the western border.

The 2.2-mile *Tower Trail,* located in the eastern portion of the forest, goes through hardwood forest, a pine plantation, and meadows to reach the crest of the peak. The *High Meadow Trail* threads through hummocky meadows and woods for 4.5 miles.

The *Ridge Trail* is the longest of the looping trails at 5.6 miles, following a winding course over the entire hill, and the *Lowlands Trail* threads through lower portions of the forest. The *Ice Age Trail,* about 2 miles long, is probably the most difficult, going fairly straight through the park directly over the peak. A number of the trails trace identical routes during portions of their length.

Degree of difficulty. All trails except the Ice Age Trail are very wide. Most have considerable slope and no paving. Some wood chip or gravel base covers the steepest portions. Steps constructed of wood ties comprise the steep final climb to the peak on the Tower and Ice Age trails.

How to get there. From I-94 in Waukesha County go south on County C for about a mile to the ranger station entrance on the left. At this writing, about a mile farther south to the left on Government Hill Road you can drive to the peak. Plans were to

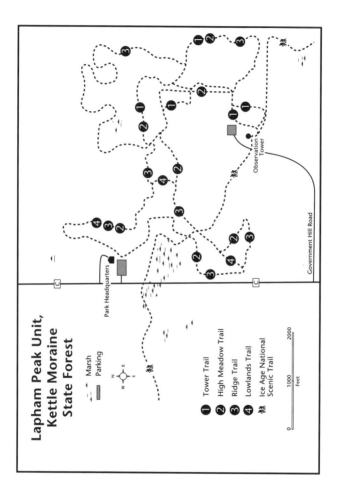

Lapham Peak Unit,
Kettle Moraine
State Forest

- ❶ Tower Trail
- ❷ High Meadow Trail
- ❸ Ridge Trail
- ❹ Lowlands Trail
- 🚶 Ice Age National Scenic Trail

Marsh

Parking

0   1000   2000
Feet

Park Headquarters

Observation Tower

Government Hill Road

close this access in 1993 and to build a new access road to the peak entering about three-quarters of a mile north of the present road.

When open. The year around from 7 A.M. to 9 P.M.

Facilities. There is parking at the forest headquarters, at a lot a short distance farther south on County C on the left, and on the hilltop. The hilltop also has a 45-foot observation tower, picnic tables, grills, and seasonal rest rooms with water. A state park sticker is required.

Other points of interest in area

The Retzer Nature Center, part of the Waukesha County Park System, has a self-guided nature trail, two prairie restoration and demonstration trails, and hiking and cross country ski trails within its 335 acres. The center staff conducts a wide variety of programs involving environmental education for visitors. A visitor center, completed in 1986, is open from 8 A.M. to 4:30 P.M. daily except holidays. From Waukesha west city limits go west on U.S. 18 about 1.7 miles, then south on Road DT a short distance to the center.

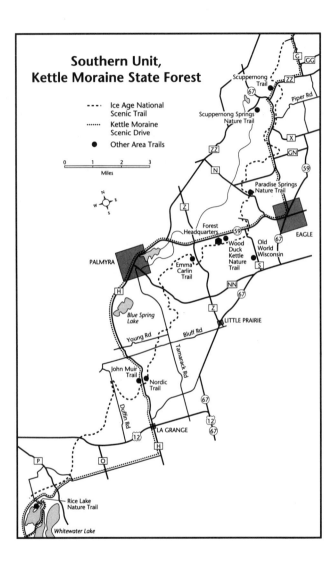

Southern Unit,
Kettle Moraine State Forest

- - - - Ice Age National
Scenic Trail

.... Kettle Moraine
Scenic Drive

● Other Area Trails

0   1   2   3
Miles

N
W   E
S

Scuppernong Trail

G GG

ZZ

67

Piper Rd

Scuppernong Springs
Nature Trail

ZZ

X

GN

N

59

Paradise Springs
Nature Trail

Z

Forest
Headquarters

59

EAGLE

67

Wood
Duck
Kettle
Nature
Trail

Old
World
Wisconsin

S

PALMYRA

Emma
Carlin
Trail

NN

67

H

Z

Blue Spring
Lake

LITTLE PRAIRIE

Young Rd

Bluff Rd

John Muir
Trail

Nordic
Trail

Tamarack Rd

67

Duffin Rd

12

LA GRANGE

67

P

Q

12

H

Rice Lake
Nature Trail

Whitewater Lake

2 Kettles, Kames, Moraines Surround You on These Trails

Southern Unit, Kettle Moraine State Forest, Eagle and Palmyra

👟 👟 👟

If a single postglacial landform—say, a moraine—can be considered a violin solo, then the Kettle Moraine State Forest is Beethoven's Fifth Symphony.

When two giant lobes of the Laurentide Ice Sheet retreated from southeastern Wisconsin, they deposited between them the Kettle Moraine. It's identified by its kettles, and also by a medley of kames, moraines, and other glacially formed features.

The kettles you'll walk among are depressions left by the melting of huge ice blocks. Kames are conical hills of gravel and sand poured with water through holes in the glacier, as in an hourglass, as it melted. You'll also follow trails over moraines deposited at the glacier's edge.

You could spend a day or weeks enjoying nature's geological orchestration in this unique 18,000-acre state forest.

Description and special features. Among the 160 miles of trails for all purposes, there are five hiking trails and four nature trails in the southern unit of the forest.

Hiking Trails

Ice Age National Scenic Trail. This longest continuous segment of the Ice Age National Scenic Trail in southern Wisconsin snakes for 32 miles from one end of the forest to the other. It enters the forest near the Pine Woods Campground at the northeast end, goes along Scuppernong Marsh and Lake La Grange as well as nearly every other major feature of the forest, and leaves at Rice Lake in the southwest end. Any of three shelters along the trail may be reserved.

Scuppernong Trail. Located in the northeast portion of the forest, the trail has three loops. The longest is 6.5 miles. It wanders into kettles and over kames, through an oak forest and several pine plantations. Enter the trail from Ottawa Lake or the Pine Woods Campground.

Emma Carlin Trail. Also with three loops, the longest is 5.6 miles. Located near Palmyra on County Z, the trail winds through meadows in beautiful rolling oak and pine forest openings. The trail is also open in winter for snowshoeing.

John Muir Trail. The longest of the three loops on this trail is 7.4 miles. Built with the help of the John Muir chapter of the Sierra Club, the trail is slightly more rugged as it passes kettles and follows moraines.

Despite objections by hiking groups and individuals, the Natural Resources Board recently opened the Carlin and Muir trails, and a connector between them, to mountain bikes. Reports indicate heavy use by bikers, especially on summer weekends. Hikers are advised to stay alert.

Nordic Trail. Specifically designed for cross-country skiing, it offers open, prairie terrain for hiking, too. Of the trail's five loops, the longest is 10 miles.

Self-Guided Nature Trails

Scuppernong Springs Nature Trail. Located in the northeast part of the forest, this 1.5-mile trail has bubbling springs, a historic trout pond built by Talbort Dousman in 1870, and the remains of a plant where marl was collected from the marshes. More than 190 varieties of plant grow along the trail and attract many bird species.

Paradise Springs Nature Trail. The asphalt paving of this 0.5-mile trail makes it accessible to the handicapped. Located about a mile northeast of Eagle on County N, the trail features a spring that flows at 30,000 gallons per hour. Catch-and-release fishing is allowed in the trout pond.

Wood Duck Kettle Nature Trail. Near the center of the forest and southeast of the visitor center, this 0.5-mile trail has 30 interpretive stops identifying flora and other features. In the spring pasqueflowers, shooting stars, and columbines grow nearby.

Rice Lake Nature Trail. At the southwest end of the forest, this 0.5-mile trail also has 30 interpretive stops. Look for bull-frogs, blue herons, painted turtles, and mallard ducks in the wetland. You may view wildlife from a blind constructed on the trail.

Degree of difficulty. Paths over kames and kettles often have short, steep pitches, but most are generally easy to hike. Trails vary in difficulty and paving. Forest management marks and maintains them well.

How to get there. Forest headquarters and the visitors' center are halfway between Eagle and Palmyra on State Highway 59 in Waukesha County. I suggest you stop there for a copy of *Visitor,* in which the Department of Natural Resources keeps forest users updated on current activities. You may enter the forest at many access points.

When open. Open from 6 A.M. to 11 P.M. daily. Campers may come to and go from their campsites at any hour. A state park sticker is required.

Facilities. While it's not considered a park, the forest has all the facilities of a multi-use state park: four campgrounds with a total of 269 sites (telephone 414-594-2135); picnicking areas; rest rooms; two public beaches; and equestrian, cross-country skiing, and snowmobile trails. Fishing and some hunting are allowed. The forest also has a target shooting range.

Other points of interest in area

Adjacent to the forest near Eagle, Old World Wisconsin illus-trates the ethnic diversity of the state in its collections of authen-tically furnished pioneer buildings brought from all corners of Wisconsin. As you wander among building clusters, you'll find this is also an excellent walking place. Open from 10 A.M. to 4 P.M. May–October, this attraction is on State Highway 67 just southwest of Eagle. A fee is charged.

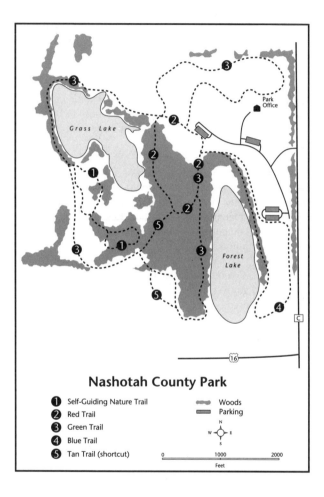

Nashotah County Park

1 Self-Guiding Nature Trail
2 Red Trail
3 Green Trail
4 Blue Trail
5 Tan Trail (shortcut)

Woods
Parking

N
W E
S

0   1000   2000
Feet

Grass Lake

Forest Lake

Park Office

16

C

3 County Park Trails Offer Strenuous or Leisurely Hiking

Nashotah County Park, between Oconomowoc and Hartland

You can enjoy strenuous or leisurely hiking at this 450-acre county park with broad trails through kettle moraine terrain. Two kettle lakes add to the natural beauty of the place, which was once the location of a religious retreat. The county has provided a variety of recreational facilities in this fully developed park.

Description and special features. Of the five trails in the park, the one-mile-long *Red Trail,* looping from the north parking lot and back, offers the most strenuous exercise over the pitches and slopes of glacial terrain. The three-mile *Green Trail* is the longest and offers the widest variety of hiking experiences as it traces the edges of both Forest Lake and Grass Lake, goes into and between kettles and over restored prairie and grassland. You can start and finish the trail from the north parking lot.

For a more leisurely walk, also along the edge of a lake and over level grassland, take the two-mile *Blue Trail* from the north parking lot. Two sections of the *Tan Trail* offer shortcuts and connectors between trails.

A *Self-Guiding Nature Trail* traces two loops through hardwood forest, oak savannah, and restored prairie. Twenty-two numbered stakes refer to an informational brochure you can obtain at the park office or the entrance booth.

Degree of difficulty. All trails except the Nature Trail were designed for cross-country skiing as well as hiking. They are wide, natural turf. Slopes vary, as indicated in the above descriptions. The Nature Trail is narrower and some parts are steeper. Builders installed steps on the steepest slope.

How to get there. About four miles east of Oconomowoc or three miles west of Hartland on U.S. 16, go north on County C for 0.5 mile to the park entrances on the left.

When open. From sunrise to 10 P.M. the year around. Fees per car are $2 weekdays and $3.50 weekends and holidays. Annual stickers for all Waukesha County parks are also available. During winter, park management posts signs prohibiting hiking on all trails except the Nature Trail to prevent interference with cross-country skiing. During my winter visit when the trails had very light snow cover, however, I found foot-tracks of many hikers.

Facilities. Full-service picnic areas include parking, large open areas, many tables, large and small grills, shelters, drinking water (except in winter), and year-round pit toilets. A few picnic tables are also located beside trails. The park also has hard- and softball diamonds, volleyball court, and horseshoe pit.

Other points of interest in area

Boating and swimming are available at many surrounding, large lakes. For more information call the Waukesha county parks department, 414-548-7801.

4 Back-Country Trail Follows Gently Flowing River

Monches Segment, Ice Age National Scenic Trail, south from Monches

This segment of the Ice Age National Scenic Trail provides an arduous, but always invigorating, hike along the Oconomowoc River. Features of the route teach the hiker how this gently flowing stream was once a wide, swift torrent that carried meltwater from the continental glacier some 10,000 years ago.

Description and special features. Beginning at the north end of the 3.4-mile segment, you will climb along a wooded ridge overlooking the Oconomowoc. When it carried the glacier's meltwater, this high ridge was the west bank of the river. You will hike through woods with many maples, making the trail especially appealing in autumn.

Descending the ridge and turning east, you will reach a sturdy footbridge and sections of boardwalk, which cross the river and nearby wet areas. The trail then turns generally south again and follows a more recent east bank near the river. Another small bridge crosses a small tributary stream. During my winter walk the quiet was broken by the thin peeping of dozens of chickadees around several bird feeders nearby.

Continuing south you will follow the border of a marshy area, part of an old millpond with muskrat houses rising above the surface. Turning west on an abandoned railroad bed, the trail ends at Funk Road near a large concrete railroad bridge.

You'll share the area with abundant wildlife, according to Ice Age Trail supporters. Owls, woodpeckers, finches, ducks and other waterfowl, deer, fox, raccoon, coyote, and squirrels inhabit this haven. In spring, you can expect to see such flowers as Dutchman's breeches, spring beauty, trillium, trout lily, bellwort, and jack-in-the-pulpit.

Degree of difficulty. Designed as a back-country trail, the path is narrow, with natural turf. Its proximity to the river would make it soggy in spots during wet weather, although board-

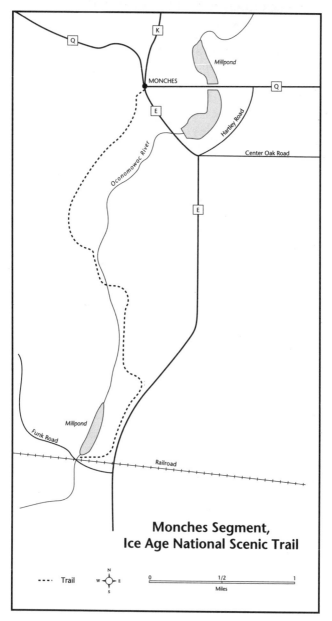

Q

K

Q

MONCHES

E

Millpond

Hartley Road

Center Oak Road

Oconomowoc River

E

Millpond

Funk Road

Railroad

Monches Segment,
Ice Age National Scenic Trail

- - - Trail

N
W · E
S

0   1/2   1
Miles

walks have been installed in several places. The trail is not level where it follows the side of the riverbank in a number of places, and numerous rocks and stones have been deposited by the glacier. While experienced hikers should not find it difficult, casual walkers may be challenged.

Yellow blazes painted on trees and a few installed signs mark the trail well.

How to get there. The north end begins at the Waukesha-Washington county line just southwest of the junction of county highways E, Q, and K near Monches. The segment ends at Funk Road about one-quarter mile west of County E.

When open. The year around. It may be impassable when snow is deep.

Facilities. None. Park off the roadway at either end of the trail.

Other points of interest in area

Monches, a hamlet with a country store, a tavern, and a restaurant, was originally named O'Connellsville by Irish settlers who had fled the potato famine. It is reported that a resident, unhappy with the Irish name, persuaded the postal service to change it to Monches, the meaning of which is uncertain. The local cemetery contains graves dating back to the 1850s.

Reference Material

For Further Reading

It's impossible to walk Wisconsin without becoming intensely curious about what's all around you—its storybook history, unique geology, and varied plant and animal life, so this reading list goes quite a bit beyond the subject of walking. A few of the books I recommend are older ones from my personal collection, some of which I acquired by combing through antique shops and estate sales. To obtain them at your local library, you may have to send the librarian into the basement or ask to explore "the stacks." But I guarantee the reading will make the extra effort worthwhile.

Alluring Wisconsin
By Fred L. Holmes
E. M. Hale and Company, 1937
   Descriptions of historically or geologically fascinating places as seen by Holmes before many of them became tourist attractions.

The Arboretum—University of Wisconsin–Madison
   Published with funds provided by the Friends of the Arboretum and other donors, this well-illustrated brochure tells about each major area of ecosystem in the Arboretum. An accompanying color map shows trails described in this book and major plant communities. You'll find it at the Arboretum's McKay Center.

The Audubon Society Field Guide to North American Wildflowers,
Eastern Region.
Alfred A. Knopf, Inc., 1979, and reprinted many times.
   This pocket-sized guide makes identification easy because it classifies wildflowers by color and includes a full-color photograph of each.

Badger Saints and Sinners
By Fred L. Holmes
E. M. Hale and Company, 1939
   Stories about both famous and little-known characters who

219

made history in Wisconsin. Holmes's writing style is colorful and entertaining.

Baraboo, Dells, and Devil's Lake Region
By H. E. Cole
Baraboo News Publishing Co., 1920–24
I found this short book in the local collection at the Baraboo Public Library. A local historian and amateur geologist and archaeologist, Cole tells fascinating stories about natural and historical features of the area.

Fitness Walking
By Robert Sweetgall
Putnam Publishing Group, 1985
Sweetgall describes a prescribed fitness program he and his partners, including a physician, developed.

A Guide to Glacial Landscapes of Dane County, Wisconsin
By David M. Mickelson
University of Wisconsin–Extension, Geological and Natural History Survey, 1983
Easy-to-read even for the layman, this soft-cover book describes and explores the origins of the widely varied landscapes of the county. Includes two drive-yourself field trips and a full-color glacial geology map.

Guide to Wisconsin Outdoors
By Jim Umhoefer
NorthWord Press, Inc., 1982, 1990
An encyclopedic work describing state parks and national and state forests, with a few trails and lakeshores thrown in. Umhoefer describes the highlights of each location, things to do there, facilities offered, and other attractions in the area.

Ice Age Lost
By Gwen Schultz
Anchor Press/Doubleday, 1974
Professor Schultz says she wrote this book after seeing a student snooze over a traditional text about glaciers. The result

is a highly readable volume that clears up popular misconceptions about the continental glaciers.

Louis Jolliet
By Virginia S. Eifert
Dodd, Mead & Co., 1961

A biography of the explorer who, with Father Jacques Marquette, was the first white man to cross the portage between the Fox and Wisconsin rivers on what is now the Marquette Trail and explore the lower Wisconsin and Mississippi valleys.

Lyme Disease, The Great Imitator
By Dr. Alvin, Virginia, and Robert Silverstein
Avstar Publishing Corp., 1990

This quick-to-read soft-cover book will help you identify Lyme disease and avoid confusing its symptoms with those of other diseases. The authors also provide information on how to protect yourself and your pets from the disease.

Madison: A History of the Formative Years
By David V. Mollenhoff
Kendall/Hunt Publishing Co., 1982

This thorough and well-documented history of Madison from prehistory to 1920 gives many new insights into the city's growth and development.

The Magic of Walking
By Aaron Sussman and Ruth Goode
Simon and Schuster, 1967

Written as walking for exercise was just beginning to become a popular national pastime, the 409-page soft-cover volume covers the subject like a warm quilt.

On the Trail of the Ice Age
By Henry S. Reuss
Ice Age Park and Trail Foundation, Inc., 1990

Text and photos in this illustrated magazine-style book describe the features of the existing and prospective routes of the Ice Age National Scientific Reserve and Trail.

Our Native Plants
By Victoria Nuzzo
The Capital Times, 1977, 1984
   Chapters in this saddle-stitched booklet originally appeared
as a series of weekly articles in *The Capital Times* newspaper.
Author Nuzzo selected only plants that are native to Dane
County and not accidentally or intentionally introduced. Each
of 119 plants is described and illustrated by a detailed line
drawing. She also tells where in Dane County to find each
plant.

The Physical Geography of Wisconsin
By Lawrence Martin
3d. ed., University of Wisconsin Press, 1965
   Everything you could possibly want to know about the subject is contained in this wonderful 608-page volume that has
been reprinted three times but changed very little from the
original.

The Places We Save
By Mary H. Maher
Wisconsin Chapter of The Nature Conservancy, 1988
   The Conservancy reveals its secret places in this beautifully
illustrated book. It's invaluable for the hiker who seeks to dis-
cover secluded trails where rare species are preserved.

A Sand County Almanac
By Aldo Leopold
First published in 1949, the soft-cover edition I own was published by the Sierra Club and Ballantine Books, Inc., in 1970.
   This conservationists' bible introduced the concept of the
land ethic to the American public. Leopold's sand county farm
is now a wildlife preserve on the Wisconsin River in Sauk
County at the southwest end of the Ice Age Foundation's "Sacred Way."
   See also *Companion to A Sand County Almanac: Interpretive
and Critical Essays,* edited by J. Baird Callicott and published by
the University of Wisconsin Press in 1987.

The Story of My Boyhood and Youth
By John Muir
Originally published by *The Atlantic Monthly,* 1912; reprinted by the University of Wisconsin Press, 1965.

The "Father of America's National Parks" records his boyhood life in Scotland, on his parents' farm at Fountain Lake in Marquette County, and at the University of Wisconsin in Madison. The Fountain Lake location is now a county park at the northeast end of the Ice Age Foundation's "Sacred Way."

Side Roads
By Fred L. Holmes
State Historical Society of Wisconsin, 1949

A man with an unquenchable curiosity about the state, Holmes said this book was in response to a survey of historic buildings. It was "all I needed to start me on another tour of Wisconsin," he said. The result is a charming collection of stories about people and places of early Wisconsin.

A Traveler's Guide to Wisconsin State Parks and Forests
By Don Davenport
Wisconsin Natural Resources Magazine, 1989

The "official" park guide of the Department of Natural Resources, this photo-decorated directory contains descriptions of all the state parks, forests, trails, and recreation areas.

Tree Walks
By R. Bruce Allison
Wisconsin Books, 1981

Arborist Allison identifies trees along walking tours of Madison and Dane County neighborhoods.

The Walker's Log
By Leslie Carola
Longmeadow Press, 1989

Spiral-bound so it will lie flat, Carola's book contains a weekly calendar in which you can record your weight, pulse, time, and distance when you walk.

Wau-bun

By Juliette M. Kinzie

Originally published, 1856; reprinted by the National Society of Colonial Dames of America in Wisconsin, 1989.

The wife of the Indian agent at Fort Winnebago (near the present location of Portage) from 1830 to 1833 writes of life on the southern Wisconsin frontier.

Wisconsin and Upper Michigan

K/H Geology Field Guide

By Rachel and Richard Pauli

Kendall/Hunt Publishing Co., 1980

This soft-cover volume describes geological field trips you can take by car throughout Wisconsin and the Upper Peninsula. The layperson as well as the student of geology will find this book easy to understand.

Wisconsin Atlas and Gazetteer

DeLorme Mapping Co., 1989

Large maps segment the entire state in exquisite detail, including all the backroads and waterways. The gazetteer has listings of campgrounds, major trails, historic sites, parks, canoe trips, bike routes, and more.

Wisconsin Sideroads to Somewhere

By Clay Schoenfeld

Dembar Educational Research Services, Inc., 1966

Schoenfeld, who was one of the state's premier outdoor writers (now semiretired), talks about fishing, boating, hunting, and the "man-land ethic."

Wisconsin State Capitol

State Department of Administration, Division of Buildings and Grounds, 1991

This sixty-page magazine-style booklet is a fully illustrated tour guide in print, providing background and history of major rooms, statuary, and paintings.

New Test Accurately Detects
Lyme Disease

There's good news about Lyme disease, if it's possible to say anything good about a disease that can, if left untreated, cause complications involving your nervous system and even your heart.

The good news is that since the development of the Gunderson Lyme Test, a blood test invented by researchers of the Gunderson Medical Foundation of La Crosse, Wisconsin, and announced in the spring of 1992, it's much easier than before to find out whether you have the disease. Previously the testing laboratory could determine only whether you had ever been exposed to the Lyme bacteria, not whether you actually have the disease. The test was subject to many "false positive" readings, often caused by bacteria or viruses of such other diseases as mononucleosis, syphilis, and Rocky Mountain spotted fever.

Later in 1992 researchers at the University of New Mexico medical school began to test a vaccine against Lyme disease on humans. Results were not yet available at this writing.

Even newer tests developed by researchers at Tufts University and at the Mayo Clinic can detect the Lyme bacterium in patients who have developed resulting arthritis.

In Wisconsin Lyme disease is most commonly transmitted by the deer tick (sometimes called the bear tick), which, in its adult stage, is only about the size of a pinhead. You can take precautions to avoid Lyme disease, but if you do become infected you can be easily and successfully cured if you start treatment early enough.

First, let's talk about prevention. Deer ticks are most likely to transmit Lyme disease from May through July and in autumn through November. In spring and summer the immature tick, or nymph, perches on grasses and low shrubs awaiting a host—animal or human—for a "blood meal." In the fall the adult tick would prefer a deer, cow, or some other animal as host, but will bite you if you are an opportune target.

As you, the unwary walker, pass by and brush the vegetation, the nymph or adult may attach itself to your clothing or skin. It is able to crawl onto your skin from your clothing, and it may clamp onto you firmly or even embed itself under your skin.

Your clothing is your first line of defense. Experts recommend that you:

* Wear light-colored clothing so you can see the tiny ticks and more easily brush them off.

* Wear long trousers and tuck them into your boots or socks.

* Wear a long-sleeved shirt and button the cuffs.

* Particularly on your pantlegs and footwear spray an insect repellent containing at least 30 percent DEET or 0.5 percent permethrin. A product such as Deep Woods Off is said to be effective. Regardless of the product you choose, it's important to read the label carefully and follow the manufacturer's instructions. Especially heed any warning not to spray certain repellents on your, or especially on children's, skin.

* Walk in the center of mowed trails to avoid brushing shrubs and low trees along the side.

* Always examine yourself carefully for the presence of ticks after walking. If you're in the woods for several days, examine yourself for ticks once per day. *The New England Journal of Medicine* has reported that the risk of becoming infected is slight if the tick is attached to a person for less than 48 hours.

To remove a tick that has attached itself to you, grasp it gently with a tweezers as close to the skin as possible and pull it straight out. Be careful not to twist or squeeze it. If you don't have a tweezers use your fingers and a piece of tissue. If a part of the tick breaks off underneath your skin, it's recommended you consult a doctor for removal. The old saw that ticks can be persuaded with a flaming match to back out of a bite doesn't work, experts say.

After removing the tick, wash your hands with soap and water and apply an antiseptic to the bite site.

How will you know if you've been infected with Lyme disease? While the Gunderson Foundation's test finally provides a definitive solution to the problem of diagnosing the disease, doctors still are often baffled by its array of symptoms. Researchers have been able to identify three stages, which were described in information distributed by the Wisconsin Department of Health and Social Services.

Stage 1: This earliest stage may bring any combination of the following symptoms: headache, chills, nausea, fever, a spreading rash, aching joints, fatigue. Without treatment these symptoms may disappear altogether, or they may recur intermittently for several months.

In about 70 percent of cases a characteristic red, circular rash appears, on the average in about ten days, but it may show up from three to thirty-two days after initial infection. Its diameter can be from two to twenty inches, with the center becoming clear. The rash may not be restricted to the bite site, and there may be more than one.

If Lyme disease is diagnosed during this first stage, it can be easily treated with antibiotics.

Stage 2: Weeks or months after initial exposure or after the first symptoms appear, some people may develop complications involving the heart and/or nervous system—heart block of varying degrees as well as meningitis, encephalitis, facial paralysis, and other conditions of the nerves. Painful joints, tendons, or muscles may also be noted.

Stage 3: Arthritis is the most commonly recognized long-term sign of Lyme disease. From several months to years after their first symptoms appear, people may experience repeated attacks of arthritis.

Research has shown that even if Lyme disease was not diagnosed and treated promptly, people who eventually received appropriate antibiotic therapy had fewer relapses than those who were never treated, the Department of Health and Social Services reports.

Obviously, when you suspect you may have the disease, the earlier you consult your doctor the better are your chances of a complete cure.

While some believe it was initially contracted by a grouse hunter in Taylor County, Wisconsin, in 1969, the disease was named for Old Lyme, Connecticut, where it was recognized in children. In Wisconsin it seems to have spread from the northwest and north central regions toward the southeast, and it is still more prevalent north and west of the Wisconsin River. About 300 cases are reported in the state each year.

Walkers who take the appropriate preventative measures and see a doctor if they suspect they've caught the disease need not let it interfere with their enjoyment of the outdoors.

How to Get a Tick Identification Card

A wallet-size card from the Gundersen Medical Foundation, Ltd., will help you identify those pesky little ticks as soon as you see them on you.

The card has full-color, bigger-than-life photos of the deer tick, which transmits Lyme disease, and its not-so-dangerous but also-a-nuisance larger relative, the wood tick. There are also actual-size drawings of the deer tick in the larvae, nymph, and adult male and female forms.

As a further identification aid, if the tick on you would fit through the hole punched in the card, it's a deer tick.

Lyme disease symptoms, and a summary of precautions you should take, are on the back of the card.

You may obtain a single card for yourself or up to 99 cards for your organization for free by sending a stamped, self-addressed envelope to the Gundersen Medical Foundation, 1836 South Avenue, La Crosse, WI 54601. For 100 to 500 cards send $4.99.

Walking Places near Lakes, Rivers, Streams, and Marshes

Aztalan State Park This former Indian fortress borders the Crawfish River.   Pp. 105–6

Baxter's Hollow Otter Creek flows out of the Baraboo Hills and through a gorge on the approach to this preserve.
                                                                  Pp. 150–52

Blackhawk Ridge An overlook provides a panoramic view of the Wisconsin River.   Pp. 69–70

Blue River Sand Barrens Located on a terrace that was once the bed of the Wisconsin River, the barrens now border river backwaters.   Pp. 73–74

Cactus Bluff Trail From the top of the bluff you'll experience one of the best views anywhere of the lower Wisconsin River.
                                                                  Pp. 166

Cam-Rock County Park A three-part park borders gently flowing Koshkonong Creek and its ponds.   Pp. 59–60

Capitol and State Street—Madison On the west loop of this walking tour is Observatory Hill, from which you'll get a truly breathtaking view of Lake Mendota.   Pp. 27–29

Cherokee Marsh Conservation Park The Cherokee Marsh and the Yahara River border this park on Madison's north side.
                                                                  Pp. 55–56

Devil's Lake State Park You'll be treated to views of Devil's Lake from the top of 500-foot bluffs on some of these trails.
                                                                  Pp. 153–75

Duck Lake Nature Trail A quiet trail bordering bottomlands near Lake Como (formerly called Duck Lake) in Walworth County.   Pp. 179–80

Geneva Lake Shoreline Path See historic mansions built by Chicago families on this 26-mile path that encircles the lakes.

Pp. 181–85

Gibbs Lake County Park The park's hillside trail follows the margin of peaceful Gibbs Lake. Pp. 143–44

Governor Dodge State Park Three man-made lakes in this park provide scenic background for six hiking trails.

Pp. 93–95

Governor Nelson State Park Madison's Lake Mendota is the focus of this urban, day-use park. Pp. 43–45

Harrington Beach State Park You can walk a mile-long beach on Lake Michigan plus a path around a 26-acre lake in an old quarry. Pp. 123–25

Honey Creek Preserve The trail follows the north branch of Honey Creek into this birders' haunt in the Baraboo Hills.

Pp. 160–61

Indian Lake County Park A trail goes nearly all the way around the park's namesake. Pp. 61–63

Janesville Segment, Ice Age National Scenic Trail The lower portion of the trail meanders with Springbrook Creek over an outwash plain. Pp. 137–39

Kettle Moraine State Forest, southern unit Trails pass a variety of lakes, streams, and wetlands. Most notable are Rice Lake; Paradise Springs Nature Trail, and its 30,207-gallon-per-hour spring; Scuppernong Springs Nature Trail with its springs and trout pond; and the Ice Age Trail, which goes by Lake La Grange. Pp. 207–9

Lake Farm County Park Early Native Americans lived by this trail along the shore of Lake Waubesa just southeast of Madison. Pp. 47–48

Lake Kegonsa State Park, White Oak Trail The park borders Lake Kegonsa, the southernmost of Madison's Four Lakes.

Pp. 49–51

Lodi Marsh Segment, Ice Age National Scenic Trail The trail follows the ridge that borders Lodi Marsh and Spring Creek.

Pp. 5–8

Marquette Trail A historical trail that runs along parts of the Portage Canal, the Fox River, and the Wisconsin River.

Pp. 13–16

Mirror Lake State Park Some of the trails follow the shore of the lake, which was formed by the damming of Dell Creek.

Pp. 167–70

Monches Segment, Ice Age National Scenic Trail The trail follows the Oconomowoc River in Waukesha County.

Pp. 213–15

Mud Lake Wildlife Area Trails lace the dry higher ground surrounded by Mud Lake and its bordering marshes in Columbia County. Pp. 23–24

Nashotah County Park Trails border two scenic glacial kettle lakes in Waukesha County. Pp. 211–12

Ostego Marsh Audubon Society's trail borders Hawkos Pond in southern Columbia County. Pp. 17–18

Parfrey's Glen Parfrey's Glen Creek, which the trail follows into the glen, is a mere trickle compared to the torrent of glacial meltwater that followed the same route and formed the gorge.

Pp. 162–65

Petrifying Springs Park Trails lace this park in the valley of the Pike River in Kenosha County. Pp. 111–12

Phil's Woods County Park You'll get a magnificent view of the Wisconsin River from the hilltop prairie on this park's trail.

Pp. 64–65

Pike Lake State Park Located on Pike Lake, a 40-foot-deep springfed lake noted for its good fishing and swimming.

Pp. 195–96

Rowan Creek Trail The trail follows a trout stream and crosses marshes via unique pontoon-supported boardwalks.

Pp. 19–22

Sugar River State Trail This 23-mile trail follows Little Sugar and Sugar rivers. Pp. 83–86

Token Creek, Sedge Meadow Trail A boardwalk provides access to a sedge meadow through which the creek lazily flows. Pp. 67–68

Tower Hill State Park Trails descend to the edge of the Wisconsin River's backwaters. Pp. 99–101

University of Wisconsin Arboretum Located on the shore of Lake Wingra, the Arboretum has one trail that follows the lake edge through a hardwood forest. Several springs along the trail flow into the lake. Pp. 39–42

White Mound County Park Trails encircle White Mound Lake in western Sauk County. Pp. 174–76

Wyalusing State Park Located at the confluence of the Wisconsin and Mississippi rivers, the park offers spectacular views of the rivers from trails on bluffs high above them.

Pp. 75–79

Yahara Heights Trail Follow this trail to a riverside Indian mound. Pp. 52–53

Glacier Leaves a Garden of Eden for Walkers

Between twenty-six and ten millennia ago, a moving sheet of ice reached into Wisconsin. At its maximum extension 18,000 years ago it covered about two-thirds of the state. The ice ground down hills, filled in valleys, and left completely new landforms in many places.

Like a giant sculptor the ice chiseled and scraped the earth. Its meltwater deposited hills and ridges. As an aside it created a paradise for walkers and hikers. You'll see its special handiwork on most of the paths and trails described in these pages.

For example, the Janesville segment of the Ice Age National Scenic Trail snakes through wide ravines created by rushing rivers of glacial meltwater. Another torrent with glacial origins helped carve the deep gash in the Baraboo Hills called Parfrey's Glen, which earlier was just a valley.

Most of the lakes and streams found by trails you'll walk were formed or greatly influenced by glacial action. It molded moraines at both ends of the Devil's Lake gorge near Baraboo to form that lake. Madison area lakes Mendota, Monona, Waubesa, and Kegonsa are remnants of the much larger glacial Lake Yahara, which covered all the area the four lakes now occupy, plus much more as the glacier receded.

Of course, the glacier deposited the drumlins seen on the Glacial Drumlin Trail in southeastern Wisconsin. It also formed the moraine over which the Brooklyn Wildlife Area Trail climbs in southern Dane County.

Even in the Driftless Area, where the glacier did not go, you'll see its effects. For example, the terrace upon which the beige sands of Blue River Sand Barrens shift and blow was the bed of the much larger Wisconsin River when it carried glacial meltwater.

Comparison of the glaciated and driftless areas of the state reveals some contrasts even in vegetation. Many plants become established in the stony soil, called *till* that the glacier deposited that will not easily grow where no ice had gone.

The Ice Age Park and Trail Foundation has purchased land or reached agreements with private and public landowners to create a trail system that will preserve and display the glacier's handiwork. When it's completed the trail will be 1,000 miles long in Wisconsin. In general, it will follow the terminal moraine of the Laurentide Ice Sheet or trace the ice's other major effects upon the land.

Much effort to set aside lands remains. While in many locales government and private interests have warmly embraced the establishment of the Ice Age National Scenic Trail, not everyone welcomes its expansion. In Dane County, for example, some landowners have resisted, expressing fears that city-bred hikers will interfere with the security and serenity of their farms. It's the responsibility of hikers and walkers to be aware of these fears and make sure they do nothing to confirm them.

Several segments of the Ice Age National Scenic Trail that have been completed are described in this book—the Janesville segment, the Sugar River Trail that follows that southern Wisconsin stream, the Brooklyn Wildlife Area trail and a portion of Indian Lake Park's trails in Dane County, the segment in Devil's Lake State Park, the Lodi segment, and, in and near Portage, the Marquette Trail. Of course, the Foundation also was behind the construction of the main trail through the Kettle Moraine State Forest. The footpath through Pike Lake State Park and the private lands south to Holy Hill are additional segments of the Ice Age National Scenic Trail in the Kettle Moraine.

I recommend the following books to learn more about glaciation in Wisconsin: *The Physical Geography of Wisconsin, Ice Age Lost, A Guide to the Glacial Landscapes of Dane County, Wisconsin,* and *On the Trail of the Ice Age.* See For Further Reading for details.

Trails with Prominent Continental Glacier Features

*Brooklyn Wildlife Area Trail The gentle hill this trail transverses several times is a moraine.   P. 57

Capitol and State Street The state capitol is located on a drumlin.   Pp. 27–29

*Certified as an Ice Age Trail by the National Park Service.

*Devil's Lake State Park, Ice Age Loop Trail Ice Age Loop Trail winds around the top of the East Bluff, which was once covered by the glacier. The Johnstown Moraine Trail passes marshes and ponds in glacier-formed kettles. The park's new trail from the Ice Age Loop to Parfrey's Glen follows the erratic strewn top of the bluff that the glacier once covered.   Pp. 154

Gibbs Lake County Park Gibbs Lake is in a glacial kettle.
Pp. 143–44

Glacial Drumlin State Trail This trail goes right through one of the nation's largest regions of drumlins.   Pp. 107–8

Governor Nelson State Park An interpretive station at the overlook of Lake Mendota on the Wakanda trail shows the borders of Glacial Lake Yahara and explains how the existing four Madison area lakes are remnants of the much larger lake that was formed by glacial meltwater.   Pp. 43–45

*Holy Hill Segment, Ice Age National Scenic Trail Traces the Green Bay Terminal Moraine from Pike Lake State Park to Holy Hill, a moulin kame.   Pp. 197–99

*Indian Lake County Park Lobes from the edge of the glacier flowed into the valleys of the park and even covered the hilltops. Indian Lake was formed in a glacial depression.
Pp. 61–63

*Janesville Segment, Ice Age National Scenic Trail The trail follows wide ravines created by glacial runoff and goes over an outwash plain.   Pp. 137–39

*Kettle Moraine State Forest, southern unit A symphony of glacial features was formed when two lobes of the glacier deposited the Kettle Moraine between them.   Pp. 207–9

*Lapham Peak Unit, Kettle Moraine State Forest A two-mile section of the Ice Age Trail goes through this unit of the forest and directly over the highest point in Waukesha County.
Pp. 203–5

*Lodi Marsh Segment, Ice Age National Scenic Trail Climb a ridge to get a commanding view of glacier-formed Lodi Marsh.
Pp. 5–8

*Marquette Trail Part of the Ice Age Park and Trail Foundation's "Sacred Way," which goes from Aldo Leopold's farm by the Wisconsin River in Sauk County to the location of John Muir's boyhood home by Fountain Lake in Marquette County.
Pp. 13–16

Military Ridge State Trail Crosses the Johnstown Moraine and an outwash plain near Verona. Pp. 97–98

*Monches Segment, Ice Age National Scenic Trail Follows the Oconomowoc River in Waukesha County. The present river occupies a much wider river valley that was formed by glacial meltwater. Pp. 213–15

Parfrey's Glen Once a valley, this glen in the Baraboo Hills was carved more deeply by rushing glacial meltwater. Pp. 162–65

Pike Lake State Park Located in the Interlobate Kettle Moraine, the park contains 1,350-foot-high Powder Hill, one of the highest kames in Wisconsin. Pp. 195–96

*Sugar River State Trail This trail borders the Driftless Area partway where an early ice sheet stopped more than 22,000 years ago. Pp. 83–86

*Certified as an Ice Age Trail by the National Park Service.

Where Native Americans Made Their Marks

Aztalan State Park The location of an enclave of Upper Mississippian Indians. They occupied it between A.D. 1100 and 1300 and left behind remains of altars and palisades, some of which have been restored. Pp. 105–6

Blackhawk Ridge Named for Chief Blackhawk, the leader of Sauk Indians who were driven from the Wisconsin territory during the Blackhawk War in 1832. Pp. 69–70

Cherokee Marsh Conservation Park Two conical Indian mounds in this park seem to be in excellent condition. One was centered on burial activity, according to a marker there. Pp. 55–56

Devil's Lake State Park Among a variety of Indian mounds in the park, built by the Woodland Culture, are effigies of a lynx and a bear on the north shore and a bird on the south shore. Pp. 153–57

Geneva Lake Shoreline Path The Potawatomi Indians, who lived by the lake, were the first to use this 26-mile path. Traces of their inhabitation are gone, but the lakeside park, Big Foot Beach State Park, was named for a Potawatomi chief. Pp. 181–85

Governor Nelson State Park A 358-foot-long panther effigy and several conical mounds, built by the Woodland Culture sometime between A.D. 500 and perhaps 1200, are located next to the Wakanda trail. Pp. 43–45

Indian Lake County Park Diggings reveal that Indians once occupied a lakeside village here. I found chips of chert, probably from Indian toolmaking, along a trail in the park's east end. Pp. 61–63

Lake Farm County Park Archaeologists have identified some 32 sites indicating Paleo-Indian occupation here as early as 5000 B.C.   Pp. 47–48

Lake Kegonsa State Park, White Oaks Nature Trail Quite far from the lake the trail passes linear Indian mounds built by the Woodland Culture.   Pp. 49–51

Lizard Mound County Park This Washington County park contains one of the largest and best preserved collections of effigy and other Indian mounds. A trail zigzags among 25 of the 28 mounds in the park, including the unique lizard, after which the park was named.   Pp. 189–90

Madison Historic Tours Of the 1,000 or so Indian mounds that once existed in the Madison area, only a few remain. Some of these are located on eight tours described here. Effigy mounds of a bear and a lynx in Lakefront Park and a lizard in Hudson Park are featured on the Schenk's-Atwood tour.   Pp. 30–32

Wyalusing State Park Several groups of effigy, linear, conical, and compound mounds in this park include one "procession" of mounds along the bluff-top Sentinel Ridge Trail. The Indian Trail was used by Indians before whites arrived. Veins of flint in rock along the Flint Ledge Trail were sources of arrowheads and tools of Indians who lived there.   Pp. 75–79

Index of Trails

What's Your Favorite Walking Place?

Is your favorite southern Wisconsin walking place included in our collection? If not, please share it with us so that we can consider including it in the next edition of this book.

Simply photocopy this form, complete it, and send to "Walking Place," Bob Crawford, 1864 Barrington Drive, Sun Prairie, WI 53590. If a map of the trail is available, please send a copy along.

Name of trail and location: _____

_____

_____

_____

Description and special features: _____

_____

_____

_____

_____

_____

Degree of difficulty: _____

_____

How to get there: _____

_____

_____

_____

_____

When open: _____

_____

_____

_____

_____

Facilities: _____

_____

_____

_____

_____

Difficulty: (See Introduction for rating system.) _____

Your name: _____

Phone: _____

Address: _____

City, State, Zip: _____